T0078393

CHANGING THE GAME

CHANGING THE GAME

10 Perspectives to Taking Charge of Your Life

LAURENS BOEL

PARTRIDGE

A Penguin Random House Company

To order additional copies of this book, contact
Toll Free 0800 990 914 (South Africa)
+44 20 3014 3997 (outside South Africa)
orders.africa@partridgepublishing.com

www.partridgepublishing.com/africa

CONTENTS

Acknowledgements

TO MY FAMILY

Where life begins and love never ends

Firstly to my parents, Walter and Gudrun Boel. You have provided me with a life one could only dream of filled with opportunities, laughter and love. You have given me a platform from which to fly high and I am eternally grateful to you both.

Mom, you have a compassion and love for me that one only hears about in fairy-tales and I take comfort in knowing that I can approach you with anything. Dad, thank you for being a constant reminder of what a great quality man should be like, you have inspired me to follow my dream as you have successfully followed your own.

My sisters, Julie and Katherine, thank you for keeping me on the straight and narrow. You have both inspired me to greater heights while still comforting and guiding me in tougher times. Julie, you have inspired me to want to become an inspirational speaker and Katherine, I strive every day to adopt your positive attitude and happiness that you exude to the world.

Lastly Stef, Katherine's fiancé, thank you for being a great addition to the family and loving my sister to the extent that you do. You are an amazing role model for me.

PARTNERS IN CRIME

Friends are the family that you get to pick and I am without doubt blessed with the amazing friends in my life. Thank you all for the encouragement and support you have shown me. Bradley van der Westhuizen, Marc-Olivier Mutwale, Chane Forte, Michelle van der Nest, Wesley Dharmalingum and Tiaan De Lange.

TO MY MENTORS

Baxolile Mabinya; my life coach and the critical thought probing master

Richard Riche; my speaking, communications and neuroscience coach

Jess Retief; my close friend and emotional intelligence coach

Sameer Parker; my career strategy coach

Steven Kahn; my neuro-linguistic programming (NLP) coach

Mauro Belotti; my integrity, respect and values based role model

John Skelton; my friend and motivator

Manesh Gokal; my sales coach

Donve Leicester; my people management coach

Conn Wood; the networking Guru

Minesh Mistry; my work ethic coach

Jason Goodall; the visionary

Jean-Jacques Verhaeghe; my attitude coach

Author's Note: Prologue

This book is a culmination of the tools and techniques that I have learnt in the pursuit of taking charge of my life. I am blessed to say that I am not the person I was a year ago. I have completely turned my life around and I am now privileged to live my dream every day. I went from being an average corporate graduate to travelling the world speaking on a global stage and loving every minute of it. I hope this book takes you on the journey that I have been honoured to take, a place where your greatness shines through and the idea of being merely average will not suffice any longer.

MY LIFE CHANGER

"Head over heels in love" – My family said as Trish and I embraced ever so passionately. I had fallen for the most beautiful Brazilian beauty you could ever imagine. She got my heart beating faster and slower at the same time and for the first time in my life everything made sense. When we were together we embodied the combination of both love and youth. It was a time of innocence, discovery and adventure. Every moment that we shared together became a nostalgic love preserved in a time that neither one of us could touch, but knew was there. It was clear to everyone around us, including ourselves, that we were absolutely enchanted by love.

Six months of absolute perfection went by before the masks of faultlessness were removed. Trish and I began to get to know the real person, not the ideal person we wanted to see in each other. This was our first rough patch, a time I would rather not remember. The next month felt longer than the previous six months combined. I look back at it now and it's a hazy mix of arguments and petty fights blown out of proportion. After the month had ended the dust seemed to be settling and I regained confidence that Trish and I would make it.

It was nearing Christmas time and in an attempt to make amends, I decided to record a special mix tape of me playing piano and singing her favourite songs. I couldn't wait, and I knew that this special gift would repair the damages of the previous month's battle wounds. She called me up while I was writing the first song for the mix tape and said; "We need to talk."

I can't remember much of the conversation after she said; "I don't love you anymore." Tears were streaming down my face. I begged her for a chance to make it up to her but to no avail, and there I was sinking deeper into a pit of despair as I put the phone down. I kicked myself for believing that this girl I had placed on a pedestal would be mine forever. She was the fairy-tale fantasy, the make believe things that I wished were true... but weren't.

I sat miserably in the chair for another two hours pitying myself... wishing the pain of rejection would somehow disappear. I felt hopeless and alone. Little did I know that this moment would be THE critical point in my life that would drive the change that I had always desired. The change to taking CHARGE of my life.

It became clear to me that my happiness was a result of my environment. If Trish was happy, then I was happy. If she wasn't happy then neither was I. I had no control over my life and I was playing into my surrounding environment's hands like a puppet. This break-up sparked a burning desire within me to become the director of my own life instead of the victim of my own story.

THE GAME OF LIFE

I was a quiet and nerdy child growing up whose best friend was my lifeless TV and PlayStation set. My favourite PlayStation game at the tender age of ten was rugby. I played it every day after school and every morning before school... I was addicted. I enjoyed playing with various teams and trying diverse skill moves. It was incredible to wield the controller in my hands and change the game merely by moving my fingertips.

I was intensely intrigued by the gaming scene as I could effect change in the game by playing it slightly differently. You see there was a glitch in the game that I played. If I were to run with one of the rugby players in a certain direction then I would always end up with the same result... that being a try. This was obviously a coding error but I still enjoyed the idea of knowing how the game worked and playing it accordingly... I could never lose.

I wondered if reality is similar to my PlayStation game. Is there a set of rules that you can follow to ensure a predictable result, or in the case of the game, a try?

At school, I did not play games during breaks because I found it hard to connect with my peers, so instead I would curiously watch the other kids. Perhaps I was stuck in the PlayStation arena but I kept looking for the glitches, the rules to the game of life. I wanted to see if there were specific ways to always win. I concentrated my observation on the popular, outstanding and interesting kids and curiously asked what it was that they did in order to be the best.

Every time I played rugby I would repeat the same move and get the same result. I watched the other kids to see what actions I could replicate in order to get the same result. The one kid that stood out above the rest was Ian. He was the ultimate master of talking to girls, and he had the unchallenged ability to engage them.

Ian had a few unfair advantages. He had crystal blue eyes, pristine blonde hair and a smile that melted every girl's heart. That, however, was not his strength. He had the confidence that no one else had at school. He would walk up to a group of girls and begin talking... something that no other guy had the guts to do.

I grabbed Ian after class the one day and asked him; "How do you have the confidence to walk up to any group of girls?" He smiled gently as his ego had been positively stroked; "I don't see them as a group of daunting girls, just a group of nice people who want to talk to me." He was undoubtedly confident, some might even say arrogant, but he did something that no one else did. He created the rules of the game that made it easier for him to win.

Instead of thinking that the group of girls were a pride of lionesses ready to pounce on any lone ranger, he saw them as a group of kind hearted, friendly girls. This motivated his ability to approach with confidence and join them in conversation. He changed the game for himself, he chose a different viewpoint and by doing so got the result that he desired.

With the life lessons of my handy rugby game and Ian's example in mind I realised that life is merely a game. A game with rules for success. I spent many hours with Ian modelling his behaviour and within a few weeks of changing the rules I was also approaching groups of girls with confidence to spare. It made sense, certain actions result in specific outcomes, just like running the same route on the rugby game would result in a guaranteed try.

With Ian's guidance I was able to learn a few rules about the game of interacting with girls, but I wondered if I could learn the rules of the game of life? Are there certain things that one must do to be successful in any area of your life and can they be learnt? This curiosity became a firm passion of mine and led to my ultimate discovery of the power of changing the game, or as I refer to it in this book, 'The Power of Perspective'.

HITTING A DEAD-END

This curiosity led me down many paths, often dead-ends, throughout my school and University adventures. It was a confusing time filled with many misunderstandings. I was aware that there was a game at play but I wasn't playing the game, rather the game was playing me. I was a victim of my circumstances. I would wake up in the mornings without any control of how the day would turn out. Within fifteen minutes of being at school, my circumstances would define how my emotions would run for that day.

If the pretty girl I was into at the time said hello to me, my feelings of pure bliss could not be disturbed. However when an irritating kid looked at me strangely a cloud of dismay and despair would hover over my day and remove the potential for happiness. I couldn't read the rules that were defining the game and therefore I was unable to play it.

None of my friends were on the same page as me. They were more curious about the female figure than understanding the complexities of human social behaviour. I also couldn't explain the phenomenon of the game to my teachers to get their guidance. It was a confusing and daunting time where I was controlled by the puppet master, life.

LEARNING THE GAME

In 2013, I joined the corporate world and I was embraced with the continued dead-end of being ruled by my circumstances. In November 2013, the pre-mentioned break-up happened and unknowingly to me it ignited the action to take charge and understand the game once and for all. The company I joined had a prestigious graduate program for aspiring leaders and I was lucky enough to be accepted.

The perks of the program were extensive, the most compelling being the constant opportunities to network with highly senior people within the organisation. I had a mind full of questions and a 20 000 company strong workforce to help me unravel the mysteries. Besides my dad, I met two of the most influential men in my life thus far; Jess and Bax.

Both men were extremely different but similar in one way... they understood the game. I spent months following them around, asking questions and modelling their every move.

After work I would read all kinds of self-help books until the words on the page would become my own. Coupled with this, I threw myself into extensively researching various emotional tools as well as spending quality time on my own to understand my thoughts.

My thirst for continued understanding led me to adopt fifteen 'top of their game' executives as my mentors to help identify myself and learn to play the game to my advantage. With this amount of support it was inevitable for me to see the glitches in the game and to play it to my advantage.

Every day since then I have thrown myself into this work in order to reallocate the resources my brain had previously devoted to alleviate the pain of the break-up. The game has become clearer on every level and my ability to model the right actions has become almost second nature. I am blessed to be seeing the results of the repeated action and my confidence is growing.

Trish drove my motivation to take charge of my life and the company was my educational vessel in which to learn.

LIVING THE DREAM

Through the implementation of the tools and techniques that I have learnt in the past year of working, I have been able to change the game in my favour.

I started as a graduate in 2013 and within two years my life has completely changed. I am blessed to say that from the start of 2015 I will be traveling the world speaking on a global stage and doing what I love every day. I have three other books that will be published by the middle of 2015 and my financial independence is becoming a reality.

Every day I wake up determined and go to bed satisfied. Before this insight I was just existing, drifting through life a slave to my environment. I am truly grateful every day that I get to LIVE WITH PASSION and create the life that suits me... changing the rules.

In all honesty it has happened so quickly that sometimes it feels like a fairy-tale. Every now and again I pinch myself to ensure that I'm not dreaming, but luckily it's true. It was definitely not all sunshine and rainbows. I went through many dark defeating times but fortunately I have been blessed with an amazing support group that constantly pick me up.

With the help of some leading thinkers and best-selling books I took the game, made it winnable and conquered it. I have taken all the knowledge I have gained and defined a formula for success. Please understand that it is a known fact that I am not a genius, I didn't know the path to success. I was just extremely fortunate to be surrounded by people who knew the rules of the game, like Ian from primary school. I had a chance to learn from them and I connected the dots in order to find techniques that would affect positive change within my own life.

Success is unique to each individual and my aim with this book is to provide tools that will help you achieve the right state of mind in order to unleash the dormant greatness that we all possess. Changing your life doesn't happen by chance, it happens by CHANGE.

CHAPTER 1

SELF-AWARENESS

THE EMOTIONAL INTELLIGENCE QUADRANT

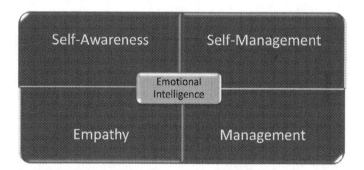

Emotional intelligence is defined as the ability to monitor your own and other people's emotions, to discriminate between different emotions and label them appropriately, and to use emotional information to guide thinking and behaviour. Fundamentally this means being aware of the way you and others around you feel, from that understanding you can use various tools to inspire a change in emotion, resulting in the right behaviour.

Centred around the self

Self-Awareness	Self-Management
Emotional Intelligence	
Empathy	Management

Centred around others

As the image above shows the first part of emotional intelligence is all about self-understanding and self-guidance whereas the second section of the quadrant emphasises the use of emotional intelligence to better relate to people and lead them more effectively. This book will only focus on the self and not how to utilise emotional intelligence to motivate others.

HELP, I SPILT MY COFFEE

Imagine that you are on your way to an important meeting. You mind is utterly focused on the objective of the meeting and nothing else is allowed to enter your mind... you are completely immersed in concentration. You run through the presentation over and over and over again in your mind, playing out every single scenario possible in order to be fully prepared.

The day of the presentation arrives and the excitement mounts. You jump out of the right side of the bed, rehearsing your smile one last time in the mirror and off you are like a bolt, taking to the streets, walking with utmost pride and confidence. 103 First Street, you have arrived.

"Good morning. I am here to see Mr McDougal." – You say oozing with confidence. "Of course sir, we have been expecting you. Mr McDougal is just running slightly late. Please grab yourself a coffee." – The receptionist kindly replies.

You march over to the coffee stand and begin pouring that traditional coffee you love, two sugars and a splash of milk. While sipping the coffee you work through how amazing this presentation is going to go and your confidence continues to soar. "There is no way you are not going to get the deal." – You affirm yourself.

Stage left enters a beautiful, independent and classy lady who immediately draws your attention. As you continue sipping your coffee, you look at her like a puppy watching their owner bringing their food, you are mesmerised. The beautiful goddess makes her way into her office and the hypnosis ends.

You continue to patiently wait for Mr McDougal and your chance to shine. As you look down to see how much of your coffee remains, a menacing coffee stain appears in your view, centre stage on your perfectly white, sparkling, buttoned up shirt; "Damn you goddess" – You mutter to yourself.

Frantically you wipe the coffee stain but to no avail, it actually just gets worse and the coffee stain is now offensive to the eye. Your confidence plummets as the visions of a flawless presentation fly swiftly out of the window. Here is where the effect of emotional intelligence can let you rise above your circumstances.

There is nothing you can do to change your reality in this case, you have no time to drive home and there are no spare shirts available... the coffee stain is prominent. The only control that you have is over the way you feel, which might not sound like a lot but the way you feel determines your behaviour in reality. The way you feel is a precursor to how you will act and therefore controls the result you see in reality.

You could spend the entire meeting worrying about the fact that you have a coffee stain, looking down every now and again enduring the inevitable reduction of self-confidence. Mr McDougal will see this and recognise your doubt and will then inherit that low confidence in you, ultimately rejecting the sale.

Another approach is to use the power of emotional intelligence to recognise the flaw but not to let it consume you. To be aware of the coffee stain and how it makes you feel but applying tools to ignore it and as a result you gain your confidence back. Let's look at the coffee stain saga, applying a more beneficial thought process. One very effective tool in changing our moods is *the art of comparison*, which is elaborated on later in the book.

We all go through hard times in our lives, feel down in the dumps and as if the world's problems are on our shoulders. I remember a particularly tough time in my first year of working. We had been given a challenging task which needed to be completed within six hours.

Our team consisted of seven people. However, three members of the team had less enthusiasm for the project than a school teacher has for late assignment excuses and another two were headed home on account of not feeling well. That left me and one other team member to finish the already impossible assignment.

The assignment was to interview twenty people from various parts of the business and compile a report on our survey. My teammate and I frantically flew around the place, begging for completed surveys. Two hours before the deadline and we had received only four completed surveys. We looked hopelessly at each other, fearing the imminent failure and the consequences of that failure.

We called up our manager, Paulina, and explained the situation; "It's hopeless Paulina!" – We sighed. Paulina grabbed us by the shoulders and took us outside for a breath of fresh air. She said; "Look across the street at the robot and tell me what you see." "A bunch of stressed out people racing to meetings." – My team mate said. "Look a little closer." – Paulina enquired again. "I see a beggar on the side of the road asking for some food." – I muttered. "Exactly," – Paulina started; "your situation is not hopeless, far from it. You are not on the side of the road with no job, family or support structure of any kind. You have already received four completed surveys... what's stopping you from getting the rest?"

We weren't overly convinced that we could get all sixteen other surveys but as we glanced over our shoulders at the beggar on the side of the road who still had hope of getting a morsel of food ... we realised that there was still hope in our situation. We looked at each other with a renewed sense of optimism and sprang into action.

Before the deadline we interviewed a total of fourteen people and compiled an extensive report. After explaining the circumstances of the team dynamics to the executives, who had given us the tasks, they were pleasantly impressed by the outcome. Paulina's small tip helped us put into perspective our problem and gave us a huge boost of positive motivation.

Comparing your situation to other people's hardships is a great way to put into perspective the size of your problem and also helps to motivate actions to overcome a seemingly massive obstacle. Let's take the example of the coffee stain and utilise the power of comparison.

In South Africa the unemployment rate is nearly 50%, which means that in a family of six people only three would have jobs. That's a frightening statistic and a statement that should already make us grateful about having a job.

The mere fact that you have a sales appointment with Mr McDougal means that you have a job and that even if this is a disastrous meeting you will still have a job after the meeting. You could quickly rush home after the meeting to get a new clean shirt and boost your confidence before your next meeting. Alternatively you could make light of the stain and how it came about and turn your embarrassing moment into a laugh. The laughing could be an effective ice breaker and ease the tension.

The obstacle of the coffee stain in comparison to the thousands of people who don't have a job and don't even have a chance to talk to Mr McDougal enables us to see that the stain is not exactly the ominous, end of the world issue that it once seemed.

Note that the coffee stain will still be there with this mind-set but at least now your focus will not be on how negating the coffee stain is but rather on how lucky you are to have the abundant opportunities you have in your life. Your confidence will not take a knock due to the negative focus on the problem and Mr McDougal will not experience the doubt resulting from destructive over-thinking and self-deprecation.

This demonstrates a very basic example of how you can become aware of limiting thoughts, and how a simple tool of changing your perspective can elevate some of those thoughts in your life to create better results.

SELF-AWARENESS

WHAT IS SELF-AWARENESS?

The day of reckoning had almost arrived... it would be the defining factor of my high school career. I had practised every day for two weeks before the test. I studied the material time and time again, over and over until the words on the book became my own, became my every thought. I had to get it right, nothing was going to stop me.

My mom dreaded my walking into the house after school as she knew she would be embraced with a request to join me on another driving practise escapade; "Please mom, I swear this is the last time." – I'd plead, though it never quite was the last time. I persuaded my mom every morning before school and every afternoon after school to practise with me in my 1992 pale blue Honda.

My senses were on high alert; every sound was heard, every movement felt and every sight seen. My hands would moisten and my mind bustled with things to remember as I inserted the key into the ignition. The motor started with its usual exhausted roar as the fearful sighs sounded from the passenger's seat; "Ok Laurens, let's take it nice and easy." – My mom said, facing the inevitable.

I frantically looked at the left mirror, then to the centre one and finally to the right mirror. I applied slight pressure to the gas pedal as the car jerked forward. My left hand tensed over the gear as my right hand felt abandoned on the steering wheel, feeling more insecure with every passing moment.

My left foot released the clutch completely uncoordinated with the right foot's downward sequence. The poor Honda felt man-handled as there was a constant back and forth swaying in motion, ending in a climatic stall. "Sorry mom." – I said, blushing. "It's ok Laurens, at least we are alive" – She replied. The lack of confidence my mother had in me depleted the little confidence that I had left. On the morning of my driver's license test I was eagerly awoken by my mom with the dreaded K53 driving instructions book firmly plastered to my head.

"It's now or never." – I sighed to my mom, slowly removing the book resting on my face. My mom and I drove in complete silence to the driving test centre forty five minutes away. With every minute that passed and every kilometre we travelled my fear grew. Finally we arrived at the dreaded driving school.

I closed the door of my mom's car and left her inside with a hopeful smile and walked towards the instructor's car. He asked me to confirm that the car was roadworthy and immediately I tapped into the long hours of diligent study that I had done in the weeks prior and performed the requisite pre-check. "Everything's in order sir." – I explained. "Let's get the show on the road." – The instructor said.

I opened the car door and concentrated on every move, diligently referring back to the hours of practise and time spent studying. My hands and feet orchestrated to the beat of my growing confidence as every move was perfectly executed. Every turn was smooth, every brake was controlled and every mirror meticulously inspected. I was in the zone, everything made sense and I was fully aware. I arrived back at the driving centre with a glee-infused happiness. I had passed my driver's licence first time.

Do you remember the days leading up to your driver's test? The amount of uncertainty and constant concentration on how to do what, when. Tapping into the memory bank of the right time to indicate, what this sign means, how many times you need to check the mirrors and in which order? Just the thought of it brings back unpleasant memories, I'm sure.

Now picture the last time that you drove your car around. How different was it to that first time? Imagine your drive this morning to work or school... Do you remember the drive in any detail? Do you remember changing the gears or flicking the indicator on before the turn? Most likely. I know that whenever I ignite the fiery engine I assume auto mode and drive without a thought of doubt.

I flick the indicator, turn the wheel and accelerate briskly without thinking about it... it just comes naturally. The state we find ourselves in when driving with this confidence and comfort is called unconsciousness. Unconsciousness is lack of awareness of what is going on around us. It is essentially an auto-pilot state. This is contrary to the feeling one gets when you are driving for the first time, or trying anything for the first time.

Reminisce about the first day of your new job, wasn't it overwhelming? There were most likely thousands of things to think about, constant challenges and with every passing minute you felt it was either sink or swim. Then two months later you kind of got the hang of it and your work became bearable and another two months later you could do everything blind folded – well almost.... When we get to that point in our lives we become comfortable, we tend to lose awareness of what is going on and we revert back to the auto-pilot mode.

This state is unfortunately how many of us go through our daily lives. We get out of bed, shower, go to work, go to gym, watch TV and then sleep... all on auto-pilot. It is estimated that over 95% of our waking hours are spent in an unconscious state. In this state we are just surviving, not thriving. We are letting life happen to us without control of where we end up.

Self-awareness combats this lack of control of our destinies and it is the connection to the conscious state. It is that awareness that you have when trying something new like learning to drive. When we are conscious in our lives we can direct ourselves onto the route we choose, we can become the directors and authors of our own stories instead of the damsel in distress or the victim.

WHAT IS THE POWER OF BECOMING AWARE?

Without self-awareness we are stuck in auto-pilot mode. Countless times I have found myself driving in the wrong direction due to lack of focus and it takes me longer to get to my destination. I miss the turn-off, stay in the wrong lane or briefly forget where my destination is.

When driving it's not the worst thing in the world to be a little late because of a lack of focus but I don't want a lack of focus to be the reason why I am stuck in a dead-end job, unhappy as can be with little to no way out of the situation. I don't want my life to be run for me, I want to run my life... don't you?

Imagine you wake up to a blissful rainstorm. You sit in ecstasy as the rain drops gently strike your roof and tranquillity absorbs the atmosphere. Lulled by the serene sound of the rain, you fall back into a deep heavenly slumber. Waking up the next morning you feel good. However, you quickly feel less rejuvenated once you spot the large ominous grey damp spot on the ceiling. "Oh NO, there's a leak!"

Adrenaline takes over and you immediately call your trusty handy-man to come right over. The doorbell rings and your heart sighs with relief; "Here is the damp spot is sir, can you fix it?" – You ask in polite desperation. "Of course, but first we have to find where the problem is, essentially where the crack in the house structure is." The same approach must be taken when solving things in our own lives, we must begin with the problem – aka the crack.

We cannot resolve things in our lives if we are not aware of the thoughts that are bringing in the negativities – the cracks, into our lives. For example if I am unhappy with life – that is the damp spot in the roof. The crack is that I am not grateful for what I have in my life and I am being dominated by comparison thoughts about others who have more material possessions than me. Without knowing which thoughts result in negative consequences we cannot fix the problem.

Self-awareness is the first step to the emotional intelligence quadrant and it allows us to see the potential problems in our lives, the cracks in our thinking. The next stage is self-management. This comprises of specific tools one can put in place to deal with the problem areas you have identified in the first phase. The handy-man would find the crack and determine from the size of the crack what approach he would need to take for a permanent solution, this constitutes the management portion of the problem.

Essentially awareness sheds light on the root areas of our lives that we are not happy with and once we understand the issues we can begin to solve them, take control of our lives through self-management tools – which will be discussed later on in the book.

Self-awareness provides an understanding of the conscious state and from there you are able to analyse your thoughts and how they manifest in reality. Then you begin with the end in mind, essentially with what you want to achieve, and you work backwards to what kind of thoughts you need in order to get it.

For example, I wanted to become a more generous person. I was earning a good salary and had more than enough money for myself so I wanted to start giving back. I was aware that every time I came to a robot and saw a beggar on the side of the road I thought he was a drunk and that's why he was on the side of the road. With that kind of thought running through my head would I have any motivation to help him?

Of course not, I would never give that person anything because they would just try get alcohol for it... so I had to change my thoughts of that experience. Instead I began to think that perhaps they come from an abusive home? Perhaps they don't have an education and cannot therefore get a job. Those thoughts motivated me to help others and become more generous.

The process begins with self-awareness, defining what you want and what is impeding you to obtain the results you desire. Beginning with the end in mind you can determine what thoughts would motivate the right behaviour and with the tools described later on fix the cracks with the appropriate solution.

You might be thinking to yourself that's an epic power, but thoughts just filter through my mind and I have no control over them. Our thoughts are based on our values and the way in which we interpret the world. When you see a person on TV who is suffering you immediately begin to think sad thoughts, putting yourself in their shoes and hoping that someone would help them, right? Maybe that's just me. That thought is manifested because human beings are caring, empathic creatures and we value other human beings.

WE CAN CHOOSE OUR VALUES

My teacher always told me that I had grown up with a good head on my shoulders, that I had good values and I believed her. I assumed that during my younger days when I was two to three years old my parents had instilled within me the essential values with which to interpret the world that I would carry through to the rest of my life.

With this limiting belief I never tried to change my values and assumed it was impossible, written in stone without an eraser. My thinking was indeed positive and well-rounded, though I was not experiencing the kind of results I wanted in my life.

At University people would run wild with racism and I would just let it happen. Anti-racial discrimination was not a value I was taught at a younger age and therefore I didn't stand up against it.

So instead of knowing I could change what was important to me, my coping mechanism to deal with the heartache was to bottle it up instead. My emotions of anger, resentment and disapproval were not only targeted at the people who were racist but also towards myself for not doing anything about it.

I strongly disapproved of the guys who treated others poorly but was unable to see past those situations and I soon began to show anger to the racists without being able to give them a reason why. This lead to a perception about my attitude to the other guys in the hostel, "He's just a grumpy dude" – They would say. I felt imprisoned, enslaved by the values, thoughts and beliefs I thought I could never change.

I held regular discussions with Jess, my Emotional Intelligence Coach, and during these discussions we debated the topic of values. He gave me an assignment which was to write down the values that I currently possessed. I worked diligently for a week straight to lay out a comprehensive model of who I am. He looked at the list and saw the intense work behind it; "Great job, Laurens."

Then he asked me to write down the values I wanted to aspire to. I didn't quite see the relevance of this at first but I did it anyway. Another diligent week later and we had the lists side by side. He then said something to me that I immediately disagreed with; "Ok, let's choose your favourite ones and begin incorporating them into your life" – Jess calmly said. "But wait, these are my values. These are the values I've grown up with." – I pointed towards the values I already owned.

"Yes those values have been incorporated into your life from a young age, but if you could incorporate values at that age surely you can re-incorporate new ones? Ones that are more beneficial, right?" It's so simple looking back at it now but before that conversation I had been brainwashed into thinking that what was important when I was younger had to remain important for the rest of my life. It was an extremely liberating process.

I went home that day literally thinking about what values I wanted, who I wanted to be. There was no longer a limit. There was no longer the looming limitation that you cannot change. I wasn't shackled thinking that I am who I am and that is final, an attitude that my teachers instilled within me. Every day we have a choice to be who we want to be, to change our value system and in doing so change the way we interpret the world.

How to become self-aware?

IT room 2-21, I entered with glee as this was the last class of my final year of studies. I took my laptop out of my bag and opened 'Fifa', as I had religiously done for the last four years. My friends ganged around me to get the picture-perfect view of the game. The nail biting game was intensified with constant oh's and ah's from my nearby fans with the teacher repeatedly glaring in my direction; "Stop bothering the other students with your stupid games, Laurens."

The end of the game was disrupted by my teacher's startling comment; "I hope you guys have started applying for jobs, it's tough out there." I looked around me as all my friends were nodding in agreement. My one friend whispered to me; "I've only gotten one response with over twenty applications. I panicked and with the disapproving glares from the support base around me I shut the game down.

I immediately opened Google and began a search... Graduate Positions in an IT firm. A large Global IT firm's home page leapt out at me and I followed their page. The Graduate Program, as the Executives referred to it, was their most prestigious offering for guys like me – having finished a four year IT degree, but my lack of confidence caused a hesitancy to apply.

I couldn't quite fathom where the thoughts of inadequacy came from and why I thought I wouldn't be good enough to be accepted into the graduate program, but they were there, heavily sapping my emotional strength and adding weight to my list of burdens.

The looming fear of a lack of job opportunities eventually forced me to apply online, though I did so reluctantly, believing it was a long shot to get accepted. "Why would they want an average guy like me? I'm not a leader." Another limiting thought that unconsciously took residence in my mind. Five minutes later I received a confirmation of application from the HR team and the rest was out of my hands. The email read as follows;

> *Dear Laurens,*
>
> *Thank you kindly for your application submission. We will contact you within two weeks to confirm your eligibility for an interview.*
>
> *Thank you for your time and have a wonderful day.*
>
> *Kind regards*

Every day for those two weeks I diligently raced through my emails and refreshed, eagerly awaiting good news, shaking in excitement like a puppy seeing its owner but to no avail. My emails consisted only of spam and emails from my dear mom. In a flash three weeks whizzed by and still I had heard nothing from the company. Panic!

My thoughts had a field day of fuelling my feelings of insufficiency and filtered over into my emotional state. It wasn't like I wasn't good enough; I had a good degree, sufficient social skills and leadership experience from my residence days but yet negative thoughts seized hold of me. I wrestled with a few self-deprecating thoughts and finally assumed that they were looking for someone with more leadership skills and that I hadn't made the bar.

Half way into the fourth week my phone rang with an unknown number on the display. "Hello, Laurens speaking" – I answered "Hi Laurens, its Jeff here. I'm calling about your application." I froze, not daring to breathe in case the breath would wake me up from this dream. "Yes Jeff, how can I help you today?" – I eagerly asked. "Laurens, I've got some good news for you."

My heart pounded in exhilaration and my mind sighed with relief. "Thank you so much for the opportunity, Jeff." – I said enthusiastically. I had been short-listed and they wanted me to come into the office park for a round of interviews to assess my eligibility and suitability for the graduate program. A thrilled persona infused my aura as my self-confidence began to brew.

The 21st of October was the day of reckoning and I entered the astonishing office park where the company resided. Together with another thirty-four candidates, we were embraced by an array of friendly smiles, gourmet breakfast snacks and a jam packed day filled with interviews and assessments.

I was extremely nervous entering the battlefield as I knew not everyone who had been shortlisted would be chosen. "Would I be good enough?" "Why would they choose me?" There were those thoughts again...

Again my thoughts were running rampage on my self-esteem and I had no control over the way they made me feel. Of course the brewing of confidence had halted as a new demon of despair arose. My disbelief that I would be chosen was amplified as they explained to us that they had received over 5000 applications and only thirty-four were short listed for a personal interview.

As you can see it seemed a trend that my thoughts were creating emotional obstacles and preventing happiness but I never quite knew how to prevent their control over me. I constantly reminded myself not to think negative thoughts but that just exacerbated more negative thinking. Every time I thought a negative thought it would be amplified with more negativity in the form of; "Why couldn't you even stop thinking negative thoughts." "It's so simple and you couldn't even do it."

These thoughts were spreading like wild fire without me being able to predict which thoughts were hindering me. From fearing rejection of an online application to limited belief in my leadership ability to finally observing my competition around me as far superior, my thoughts were hindering my actual potential. My thoughts were the director and I was just the puppet accepting orders from above.

Fortunately for me, my self-limiting thoughts did not cost me the opportunity to begin working for the magical Global IT firm, as I, along with thirteen others, were offered positions. I am sure that many of the other candidates were experiencing the same limiting thoughts that I had. The other twenty-three candidates were politely rejected as the rest of us were overjoyed knowing that the competition had been fierce.

And so we began the adventurous year with an introduction from the Chairman and Founder of the company. He inspired smiles across the room as he said; "This year is about learning. You will be given access to anyone in the company to ask questions and to learn from." My hands gripped each other as a devilish delight caressed my face; "I have over 20 000 people with experience to learn from at my fingertips, surely someone can help me with direction." – I gleefully whispered to myself.

Although at first it seemed daunting to achieve the objectives laid out for us for the year's program the hardest part was dealing with the other graduates and the imminent group dynamics. I was constantly prey to limiting thoughts and envisioning negative scenarios and I couldn't seem to stop myself.

I became obsessed with imagining terrible scenarios in the hope that I would be well prepared to react to them, it was definitely not healthy. I wanted to be a well-oiled machine radiating with confidence but I didn't know where the cracks were in my ceiling and I had no idea how to solve the problems. I was easily influenced by the other graduates and they had no problem taking advantage of that fact. After six months of high-school like games and cliques I had almost had enough – next week was going to be the deciding factor; do I stay or do I leave?

We were just about to start a new rotation in a different area of the business, one that I was thoroughly looking forward to. This area of the business was made up with the mavericks and undisputed entrepreneurs of the company. I was excited as I assumed there would be less political games entrenched in the teams. Our first meeting was with a fellow named Jess Retief who had an astonishing way with people.

I remember him interchanging masks between conversations and like a chameleon changing his social approach depending on the person and the objective of the conversation. To the graduates he spoke like a surfer dude straight off a wave and to the Executives he spoke with authority and conviction so that they would buy into his ideals. I should not have been surprised at his amazing people skills as he was the psychologist of the company.

He explained, in a group presentation, the significance of our thoughts and how they manifest into reality. He explained that the thoughts we produce are not based on reality but rather on how we interpret reality and that we are able to choose thoughts that are more empowering. It was as if he had tailored the presentation directly at me because I had been feeling like a slave to my thoughts, dearly needing an escape.

After the meeting I awkwardly waited around for Jess feeling scared, confused and not sure of what to say. I grabbed him as he left the training room and asked him for his help. "I'm not sure who I am and I would like to find out." – I fearfully stated, thinking he might judge me... but instead he delightedly accepted my gesture and said; "This is going to be fun."

We began the next day bright and early at seven am in his office; the turquoise-blue tinted training room, number four. The room consisted of lecture-like seating arrangements, exposed windows revealing the clear pristine African sun. A steaming cup of coffee was waiting.

Jess entered at ten past seven as he was caught up in a quick discussion with a needy employee. He smiled as he saw me eagerly awaiting his arrival and said; "Great, let's begin." He told me that the key to understanding yourself is first to listen to yourself.

"Picture the last class that you attended," – Jess began, "if the teacher was busy explaining the work and you weren't listening, did you understand how to do the homework when you got home?" "No." – I replied. "Of course not. You might have spent a few minutes to understand that work but it took some diligent self-study to get there. The same applies to ourselves. We must first listen to ourselves before we can understand ourselves."

He explained that my thoughts were like the teachers I dreaded in school and that listening to them gave me great insights into understanding who I am. Jess explained that we are so unconscious with our thinking that we don't even know what we are thinking most times. "Do you remember what you thought when you first entered the training room twenty minutes ago?" I couldn't answer but his point had been made.

We go through life being slaves to our thoughts and in so doing getting results that we may not always desire. Becoming aware of the thoughts/cracks allows us to resolve our reality, fix our leaking roofs.

The unconscious state, often experienced when we are driving, then guides our lives. If we are not aware of our thoughts then our destination will be unknown. Often we will find ourselves in a trench with a shovel hidden under a foot of dirt. Instead of trying to find the shovel we obsess about shouting out for help, trying to climb out ourselves and are met with failure and disappointment leading to despondency. That is when we find ourselves blaming the world for our shortcomings and we remove the power of solving our own problems.

Tony Robbins, NLP genius and world-renowned peak performance coach, said; "We are the only ones standing in our way." Fancy a doctor prescribing cough mixture to fix your exasperating cold. Can the doctor force you to take the medicine that will make you feel better? Of course not, all the doctor can do is prescribe the medicine but it is up to you to take the medicine.

You are in complete control of your life, and as you begin to own that knowledge you begin to empower your motivation to get out of life what you want. As the age-old saying goes; "You can lead a horse to water but you cannot make it drink."

We are governed by our thoughts, no one else's. Sometimes people's thoughts manipulate our thinking and it feels like they are controlling us. Your thoughts are owned by you, and therefore you can take control of the outcomes in your life. It is our choice to, as Les Brown, world famous Inspirational speaker, always says; "Be in our way or to be ON OUR WAY."

Through Jess I learnt to become self-aware, which is the first step to understanding and influencing your thoughts. He provided me with a fun way to learn self-awareness and I would like to teach you the same process.

Imagine that you are playing a game for the next five days and the game is called "The Game". Whenever you think of "The Game" or the "The Game" crosses your mind you must stop what you are doing and just listen to your thoughts.

If you are sitting at home watching TV and your dad rushes into the room screaming with delight; "We won our golf game!" The word 'game' in the sentence could trigger you to remember "The Game" and before listening to the result of your dad's victory you can quickly listen to your thoughts.

Its sounds very simple, right? The cool thing is that self-awareness is that simple, it is listening to the thoughts that are running through your mind and realising how these thoughts manifest in reality. For example, if I have thoughts of discomfort or anger my body will react with folding my arms and turning away from the situation.

If you are aware of the reaction whenever your arms are folded, you can listen to our thoughts and see what is bothering you... is it something you can change? Is it something you cannot change? If you can change it then 99% of the time you will but if you can't change it then you can begin using the tools described later on to deal with the negative emotions and get yourself back to a state of contentment.

I know that playing this game may seem arbitrary but it's an easy trick to learn how to access your thoughts. Once you get the hang of it, it's like riding a bike... you never forget it.

Taking charge of your life begins with becoming self-aware. Every decision that you make results in the life you have now, and your decisions are based on your thoughts. It is all up to you, it is no one else's way but your way.

[See exercises for this chapter at the end of the book]

Chapter 2

IS IT HELPFUL?

We all want greatness for ourselves and to live a happy and fulfilled life but if it was that easy then everyone around us would be doing that right? Looking around my office I see just how rare happiness and fulfilment is. So many of my colleagues go to a job that they hate, a job that is causing them to be sick... they are committing spiritual suicide. Selling their soul to the corporate world for promises of higher pay and less time in which to enjoy the money.

The people I coach on a daily basis are all able to talk about how hard their lives are and how they wish their lives were better, but that's all they do... wish. They are all well aware that they have greatness within them yearning to shine but excuses are their only form of action; "I don't have the time." "I don't have the money." "I don't have the skill." Well of course not, no one is born into intelligence, success or fame. We have to work at greatness because it doesn't just land in our laps.

No one who has changed the world was born with special abilities over you, they only had fewer excuses holding them back from their greatness. What we need to master is to empower positive perspectives and act on specific goals aligned to the greatness we desire. You know that you are worth more, worth greatness and now is the time to take action... do what others won't so that you can live the life that others can't. Success is inevitable with ACTION.

WISHING WITHOUT ACTION IS JUST DAYDREAMING

Eleven pm on a cold South African winter's evening, the wind howling outside. "I shouldn't be at the office anymore." – I sighed out loud in frustration as the rest of the team ignored my cry, wishing the exact same thing. A few minutes of silence followed until Jean, my team mate, responded; "We are never going to finish this presentation in time."

Our manager Lauren, who was sitting in the room next door, came out at the sound of the ruckus and asked what was going on. We all sat like children in detention and everyone kept quiet. She said; "That's more like it!" And stormed back into her office trying to finish off her mountain of work.

We sat in frustration, unproductively hoping that Lauren would come out and approve our departure from the wretched work place but to no avail. It had just reached midnight and none of us were even looking at our computer screens anymore. Candi had fallen asleep, Caitlin was engrossed in angry texts to her mom and Jean and I were playing thumb war.

Caitlin's conversation with her mom was reaching a climax and with one final upsetting reply from her mom, Caitlin jumped up and shouted; "I can't take this anymore!" Lauren rushed out of the office hearing the high-pitched scream.

Caitlin, in a complete rage, said to Lauren; "I'm going home, I can't take this anymore. Goodbye."

She stormed off without giving Lauren a second to contemplate stopping her. After the dust had settled Lauren returned to her office and the rest of us returned to wasting time hoping she would eventually relieve us of our duties. Six am was around the corner and finally Lauren gave us permission to leave. It was useless attempting to resolve the anger we had towards her as we had to be back in the office at nine am. "I'll just grab a shower and come back" – Jean sighed.

Caitlin entered the office with a great big smile on her face at nine am, as she at least had a few hours of peaceful sleep. She looked at us and could see the lifelessness in our demeanour; "Don't tell me you guys stayed the whole night?" We all nodded collectively in despair. Caitlin was bewildered at our lack of initiative to stand up to Lauren.

"Didn't you guys want to go home?" – Caitlin asked, to which we responded; "OF COURSE, YES!" "So what did Lauren say when you guys asked her?" – Caitlin asked. We all looked at each other sheepishly; "Uhm, we didn't ask her." Caitlin shook her head and said; "No wonder you guys stayed here this whole time." Caitlin took pity on us and felt lucky that she had some sort of emergency to sort out and that Lauren had been unable to stop her.

Caitlin then told us that this morning Lauren hadn't even been angry, she politely asked her if everything was ok and if there is anything that she can do to help. Lauren was very understanding and it's really because Caitlin asked for what she wanted. Caitlin sat down, preparing to begin work again when she offered her last bit of advice; "Wishing without action is just daydreaming."

Imagine yourself sitting in your car with the key in the ignition but not yet turned. Until you turn the key the car won't move no matter how much you wish it would. With action you are able to effect change in reality. This chapter outlines the initial steps needed to take action, and having a clear vision or plan of action.

So before moving onto the next chapter you must be certain that you have figured out where you see yourself in one week, month, years' time... you need to know where you want to go before you can begin travelling. Ensure that you are fixing the right crack and not wasting your time repairing something that is not going to solve the problem of the leaking roof.

This chapter will help you determine what cracks need fixing and the next chapter, 'Making your Change Last', will provide you with actionable steps to turn the leaking roof into the state you desire it to be. Start with the vision, then map out the way to get there.

We need both vision and action to make a difference in the world, as Nelson Mandela famously said; "Action without vision is only passing time, vision without action is merely daydreaming but vision with action can change the world." Let's start with the cracks and determine which perspectives motivate the right behaviour.

IS IT HELPFUL?

Make sure that you are comfortable with your new found ability of self-awareness which you practised in chapter one with the exercise "The Game". Once you have conquered the art of accessing your thoughts, knowing where the crack in the roof is, and relating your feelings to a logical statement, the next step is to deal with that thought.

The issue that most people have once they have discovered the thought creating the crack in their lives is that they immediately judge the thought, over-analysing it to a point where it destructs their self-esteem. This instant judgement prevents the brain's creative juices from solving the problem as all the resources of the brain are obsessing over the terrible thought and its origins. This leaves you in a helpless state, like a rocking chair; giving you something to do but not getting you anywhere.

Unfortunately we are the biggest critics of our own actions... have you ever noticed that? We are able to give positive and empowering advice to our friends who have made mistakes but when it's our own actions that we are analysing we tend to be overly critical and destructive.

Preaching not practising

My sisters and I have a fairly substantial age difference of four and six years respectively, me being the youngest. It might not seem like much when you are in your twenties but before University I always assumed the role of the irritating immature infant and therefore I was never invited to any of the parties that my sisters went to. They had their own friends and I had mine, there was no sharing.

When I had finally left University and the stage of annoying brother withered away I began to connect with my sisters and their friends on a much deeper level. Both Julie and Katherine would invite me to hang out with their friends and join the parties. This was hugely beneficial to my development as I was surrounded by older, educated people who had their lives figured out... or so I thought.

I used the interactions with my sister's friends as my personal laboratory in an attempt to understand human psychology a bit more. One particular night out with Julie and her close group of friends was an eye-opening experiment for me. The assumption I had made that the older you are, the more you have it together was completely thrown out the window.

Julie's friend, Rene, was the loudest and proudest of her group. Rene made sure that everyone could hear her over and above the ear deafening beats that the DJ was playing. Whilst enjoying a casual drink in the relaxed smoking bar Rene's voice penetrated my hearing as she came running up the stairs, laughing with pleasure. She joined the table and instantly all eyes were on her.

She began telling the story of her friend, Susan, who was having such a hard time with her boyfriend; "She's staying with him even though he treats her like rubbish. I wish she could see that she deserves better than him and that she doesn't need him in order to be fulfilled!" – Rene preached.

I looked at her in amazement as that was very sound advice, something that I thought I would be greatly appreciate if I were in Susan's situation. Rene continued giving her opinion of Susan's situation as I found myself nodding in agreement to everything she said;

"She must find happiness within herself not get it from someone else."

"Rather be alone and happy than with someone and miserable."

All golden pearls of wisdom. I had gotten a picture of Rene's personality, from a few brief interactions that night and formed the opinion that she is confident, assertive and knows her worth. She has it together.

The drinks continued to flow as my experiment entered a new phase of observation, how do people react when induced with lethargic alcohol streaming through their blood? Everyone went into a state that can only be described as divine, the music was pumping as well as the fists of everyone in the group... except for Rene. She was sitting on the couch, looking enviously at everyone executing rhythm-less movements on the dance floor. This struck me as weird as she was in my mind the confident 'Who cares? Have fun!' kind of girl.

I grabbed Rene at the bar to begin a quick investigation; "What's wrong Rene?" – I asked sincerely. "Ag nothing really, there was just this random guy that came and talked to me... he was really ugly and made me feel bad about myself." – She said slurring ever so slightly. This put a dent in my impression of her, maybe she wasn't the confident girl I had imagined I thought to myself.

Midst conversation Rene was dragged away by the bar tender to place her order. Julie quickly came over to try lure her favourite dancing partner, me, back to the arena of fun. I said; "I'll come just now Jule's, I'm just helping Rene with some guy issue of hers." Julie's face turned upside down and with an indifferent tone she said; "Don't worry about her, she always has guy troubles." – She said, running back to her friends.

I had assumed that perhaps Rene had had a little too much to drink and therefore overreacted to the guy who mistreated her... but from what Julie said about her it seems that that's just the way Rene is, her regular character. I happily left my experiment and found myself back at the arena of happiness and endless possibilities, the dance floor.

Two months after the festive party and three more interactions with Julie's friend Rene brought home what Julie had said in the night club. Rene was always having issues with guys and almost always because they were mistreating her. I found this intriguing as Rene was undoubtedly the best advice giver in my sister's friendship circle but was unable to put to practise what she preached.

Whenever a friend in need appeared in Rene's aura she would jump into positive puppet mode, giving encouraging, boosting and powerfully persuasive comments that would cheer anyone up but when she analysed her own life the positive puppet would revert to a negative Nancy focusing on the one thorn amongst the roses.

We are always way more critical with ourselves than with other people. We have a remarkable ability to comfort and advise our friends to get out of the relationships that are causing unhappiness but when we find ourselves in the same destructive environment, the positive, empowering and logical statements vanish.

Rene is a prime example of this phenomenon, she is able to advise her friends with pearls of empowering wisdom but her wisdom is wasted on herself because self-deprecation rules.

Instead of trying to understand the situation, what her thoughts are and how they could be more empowering... Rene immediately jumped to "Obviously I am not good enough." The focus of the mind is then on beating herself up instead of on the thought that is causing her insecurity.

She is blaming the open window for the dampness on the ceiling instead of the crack itself.

This judgement of ourselves clouds our vision to see the thought that is provoking the unwanted result in our lives. What we need to do is prevent the judgement from occurring so that we can discover the crack and deal with it. To stop the destructive spiral in its track we can change our way of thinking about the problem by asking a very simple question.

THE HELPFUL QUESTION

When you are analysing your thoughts it can be easy to go straight to

'Why am I thinking that?'
'No wonder my life is bad!'
'Is it all my fault?'
'Why can't I lose any weight?'

"Ask and you shall receive." Your mind will answer the discouraging question with a discouraging answer;

'You deserve it, that's why.'
'You're fat because you're a pig.'

Which only adds fire to the flame of self-doubt. Dealing with negative thoughts is hard enough without the added pressure of constant self-deprecation.

We lose the power to analyse our thoughts if we immediately blame ourselves for having them. The analysis deviates from a point of trying to understand, to a judgement battle which only leads to critical self-destruction. How do you stop this? A simple trick that Jess taught me to not self-destructively analyse thoughts is to ask a question when a seemingly negative thought pierces your mind. "Is this thought helpful in what I am trying to achieve?"

The concept of asking if it is helpful has huge psychological advantages. Firstly the way in which the question is positioned removes the automatic assumption that the thought is ridiculous, on the premise that depending on a different situation that thought might be helpful.

This slight change in mind-set will remove the default judgement that we have when analysing thoughts, the 'what a stupid thought'. The question changes the focus from judgement of the thought to determining if there is another thought that is more helpful in this specific scenario.

Let's make this concept a little more tangible. Imagine a situation where you are sitting opposite a kind-hearted elderly lady with a gentle smile that melts your heart. You are the only two people in the public library gently conversing with irregular eye glimpses. I think we can all agree that the thought "I AM IN DANGER." Would be less than helpful in this specific situation.

Our traditional analysis of that thought would lead us down the road of,

'How could you think that?'
'What is wrong with you?'
'You're stupid for thinking that!'

This removes the eagerness to try and understand and then replace the thought with an empowering one for the moment at hand. When asking is it helpful in this situation one can say no and replace it with another thought knowing that in a potentially different situation that thought would be valuable. Instead of obsessing on how stupid the thought was your mind looks for a more positive replacement thought.

Imagine yourself in the same public library opposite the ever kind elderly woman enjoying a good read. Books begin to fall off the shelves as the table trembles. You look over to the elderly woman and her eyes widened as if she has just seen a ghost. Both your expressions turn into fearful terror as you hear a frantic scream from outside; "EARTHQUAKE!" I think that in this situation the thought "I AM IN DANGER." would be suitable.

In essence we are trying to teach ourselves to be nicer to ourselves. Not to jump to the immediate worst case scenario, enduring the relentless eroding of our self-esteem but rather to engage the situation and determine which thought would be more beneficial.

We can force ourselves to not judge our own thoughts but allow ourselves the permission to analyse them and understand the root cause, the crack, so we can repair the crack and remove the dampness.

This is the precursor to using the perspectives defined in the next chapter. If you are able to determine that a specific thought is not helping you achieve your goals in a situation, you are empowered to choose another perspective that could help you achieve your goal or at least make you feel good. We must use self-awareness to locate the crack in the ceiling, ask if the thought is helpful in achieving our goals and replace these thoughts with helpful perspective changes... change the phone from an alarm clock to a calculator depending on your need.

REPAIRING THE CRACK

Using the simple technique of asking the question; "Is this thought helpful in what I am trying to achieve?" when a negative thought appears will help you determine where the cracks are. Your focus will not be on why the thought occurred but rather on whether there is a more helpful way to think about your current situation. Once you have found the crack you can replace the negative thought with one of the ten perspectives defined below that will help you achieve the motivation to act.

To only find the thought that is not helpful in the situation is half of the battle won. The next step is fix the problem, so that it doesn't affect your life. Now is the time to take action.

THE COO LESSONS

Henry is the COO of the Group Holdings Company, where I worked, and I'm also blessed to say that he is one of my mentors. At our first meeting he asked me to come prepared with questions about what I wanted from the mentorship relationship. I thought long and hard about what to say, the only motivation that came to mind was that he is just the most energetic executive I had ever met.

He was quite young to have progressed so far up the corporate ladder, at only forty-two years old and his enthusiasm and excitement were unmatched in the company. The day that I met Henry I thought I could work for the company for a long time, his passion for the company awoke passion within me. He spoke to the graduates about the strategy and vision for the company going forward, a topic that most of us prepared ourselves to nap through but instead none of us dared blink for fear of missing one of his riveting stories.

He didn't discuss the company's revenue or acquisition plans in America but rather told stories about the crazy moments he has experienced with the company and some of the moments he has had to endure with them as well. He was able to relate to and engage with a bunch of graduates like no one else I had seen in the company and that was why I wanted him to be my mentor.

I made sure to come up with a few more concrete reasons for his mentoring before our meeting, such as visioning techniques and goal setting in order to give him an idea of what I expected from our brief visits. I waited patiently and anxiously outside Henry's office until he asked me to enter. I could feel a rush of emotions as I stepped into what seemed like an infinity office. His office size was like his energy, COLOSSAL.

We started off the discussions with small talk and light introductions as I sneakily introduced the real reason why I wanted him to mentor me; "I admire your energy Henry, and I want to surround myself with energetic go getters." He smiled genuinely and agreed to show me the ropes. This was one of the most exciting moments of my life as a true role model of mine had agreed to take me under his wing. I was feeling on top of the world.

I was only able to schedule one thirty minute meeting with Henry every second month so I made sure that I was prepared at each meeting, ensuring I would absorb the most I could from our brief interactions. During November, our third meeting, I had been having some problems with the stringent admin systems in place and found that more often than not the system impeded productivity.

I explained my frustrations to Henry about the inflexibility of the company, and that each minor change needed to go through six people or more before it could be approved. I am creative and love to improve the way things are done but I felt it was stunting my growth and value that I could add. Henry eagerly listened as his passion lay in improving the company's operations as well as helping young people grow. He politely waited until I had completely finished moaning and began a rebuttal.

"I understand your frustrations Laurens, unfortunately when a company gets to the size of our company you have to have processes in place. We have learnt the hard way that certain business procedures need to follow processes. I promise that these processes were defined because they made things easier at a time... I'm not saying that they are still relevant and that's where a young fresh minded individual like yourself can thrive and help the company move forward."

I thoroughly enjoyed interacting with Henry as most of what he said and how he said it was positive, motivating and empowering. He never thought a question was stupid and never thought of using his authority to make things relevant. "Why has the company become so strict?" – I asked.

Henry paused briefly and replied in an earnest tone; "People have found chinks in our armour. If a company finds a weak link in its way of doing business but doesn't do anything to fix it then that weak link will remain in the chain." I nodded in agreement, though I still felt that the way I wanted to do things should have been obvious and that the strict rules needed to be relaxed.

Henry did make a very good point when saying that if a problem is not fixed, only identified, it doesn't go away. When you find a thought that is not helpful in a situation it must be acted upon, it must be changed otherwise the problem will persist. To merely find the crack in the roof doesn't stop the dampening of the ceiling at the next rain fall... you need ACTION to fix the problem.

The honest solution to replacing unhelpful thoughts is through trial and error. You can notice a crack that needs attention and apply the various perspective changes that are defined in the next chapter, it is up to you to see which perspective provides a helpful alternative way of looking at life. Everyone is different and therefore not every perspective is helpful to other people.

Ok, so I have mentioned perspective changes a lot already and I haven't yet touched on what they mean, don't worry about that. As long as you understand the principle of finding the cracks that need attention.

Starting with self-awareness you become aware of your thought pattern. By filtering them through the 'Is it helpful question?' you can determine which thoughts produce the crack in your life and lastly you can apply one of the following perspectives to 'fix' the crack.

Now the fun part, using some emotional intelligence tools to change the thoughts limiting your life.

[See exercises for this chapter at the end of the book]

CHAPTER 3

THE 10 LIFE-CHANGING PERSPECTIVES

"People are always blaming their circumstances for what they are. I don't believe in circumstances. The people who get on in this world are the people who get up and look for the circumstances they want, and, if they can't find them, make them." – George Bernard Shaw

WHAT IS PERSPECTIVE?

Perspective is defined in the dictionary as *a particular attitude towards or way of regarding something; a point of view*. Perspective is therefore the way in which we see the world. We perceive reality and create context to understand that reality, which is a perspective.

Do you agree that there is a big difference between a house and a home? I often walk into someone's house and get that feeling that I have arrived at home. The house is welcoming, the bedrooms embody relaxation and the atmosphere is comforting... *'Home sweet home.'* Then there are times where I walk into a house and experience the overwhelming feeling of disappointment as if I had just entered a dark, dingy dungeon.

My mom and I have always had differing views on the house vs home debate. I have always found my apartment to be *home sweet home* worthy. As you enter our apartment you are bombarded with a sensory blast; from different colour couches, to surplus amounts of gadgets and perhaps a t-shirt lying here and there.

I walk into this house and immediately I feel at *home,* though when my mom enters the apartment home is the furthest thing from her mind. She sees the coloured couches as not fitting into the design of the room, the gadgets that should be packed away and the t-shirts folded up or thrown out.

That is the concept of perspective, we may all see the same thing in reality, the same couches, gadgets and clothes but the context from which we view that reality and the perspective we adopt differs from person to person.

THE TAXI RAGE

I was driving to work the one day, the sun was shining, birds were singing and I thought this was going to be a picture perfect day. That's when a Taxi decided to prove me wrong by pulling off from a side road to push in right in front of me and slow me down. This infuriated me as these Taxi drivers just don't care about the law or anyone else on the road. In a rage of irritation I hooted my horn and flashed my lights but to no avail, the Taxi driver just smiled and carried on his merry way.

I arrived at work in a huff as my co-workers avoided contact for fear that I would rip them to shreds. One of my colleagues mustered up some courage and asked me what had happened? After explaining the ordeal they all sympathised with me as they too have been the victims of poor driving, especially when Taxis are the culprits.

My one co-worker, Candi, then said; "That's not ideal Laurens, sorry. I guess these Taxi drivers get tired and frustrated driving eighteen hour days with little pay and cutting corners helps them make ends meet."

Everyone paused for a brief moment as they contemplated Candi's statement. She had completely turned my scenario on its head by viewing the situation not from the victim's standpoint but rather through the eyes of the perpetrator. I looked at her and nodded in agreement as a soothing gentleness instilled my body, making me feel better.

It was amazing how Candi was able to see the exact same situation from a fresh perspective. A perspective not tainted by the polluted position from which I viewed the scenario. She looked at the perpetrator as a human, with human emotions and I was able to connect with that. I pictured myself driving eighteen hour days in the blistering hot African sun and thought the Taxi drivers are actually not that disgraceful.

There are different ways of the perceiving the same situation. Sometimes the way we see it makes sense but does it make us feel good? It makes sense to see that the Taxi driver is breaking the law and getting in my way but all that does, is make me feel offended and helpless. Looking at it from Candi's perspective allowed me to rationalise the situation from a different angle. Her point of view was also valid and helped lessen my feelings of discomfort.

At least with the new perspective I was able to feel better. Let's face it... it doesn't matter how angry or happy I am it doesn't change what happened and it certainly doesn't change the way the Taxi driver feels or behaves. The only thing that I can change and have control over is how I choose to see the situation.

I am always puzzled about how people can have different perspectives on the same situation. How was Candi able to see the same thing that I did in a different way? Surely a Taxi driver is seen the same by everyone... or so I thought. This ability of some people to see reality from different angles sparked an intense interest in me, and so began my escapade of observing people, trying to understand how their perspectives differ from other people and why.

THE PENSIONER VS THE RISKER

Our perspectives are historically determined by our backgrounds, experiences and values. My dad for example perceives any financial risk as out of the question because he is sixty years old, on pension and has little chance of recovering from a financial catastrophe.

My dad started his own business when he was around thirty years old and took numerous risks along the way, received a few rewards but also saw the dark agonising side of risks gone wrong. With that mind-set you can understand why my dad feels the need to protect me from the potential heartache that risks contain by advising me to play things safe.

I, on the other hand, am only twenty-four years old with the world as my oyster. I have little fear of risk as I still have the rest of my life to recover from any disaster and currently have no responsibilities like; family, mortgage... My dad and I will forever always have a different view on life. He is currently in a pensioner's paradigm while I'm living care-free in my happy go lucky youngster phase. What we have been through in life changes how we perceive our reality and therefore changes our perspective on life.

As you can see my dad, mom and I have differing views on life due to our different backgrounds, experiences and values. These differing views are our perspectives of life and I hope that by the end of the chapter you understand that you can choose your perspectives, instead of being enslaved and governed by your past.

My clients immediately agree that changing perspectives has the ability to change their lives but they always ask me the same question; "Laurens, that's great for some people, but I can't change the way I see my life. I've been living like this for too long, I don't know another way... I'm just an old dog that can't learn any new tricks."

I have to agree with them to a point. We have all grown up with various values that are indoctrinated within us and it's not so easy to just change the way we view the world. But, what if I tell you that you already change perspectives every day without even realising it?

THE CELL PHONE MUTATION

Do you agree that we can view the same object from a variety of perspectives?

Imagine sitting down at your favourite restaurant with a quiet jazz song in the background and drinks awaiting your arrival. Your friend thanks you for coming and you begin to indulge in amusing small talk. In the midst of an entertaining joke being told by your friend you hear your cell phone ringing, it's not an urgent call but you still need to answer it. In that case your cell phone is seen as a traditional communication device.

After the fantastic dinner you retire home and pamper yourself to some well-deserved sleep. Your sleep is enhanced by an enjoyable dream and just before the climax where you are crowned the king of your own story the most annoying noise pierces your ear drums and its six am, time for the real world again. Now you see your phone as an infuriating alarm clock.

While sleepily getting out of bed you open the morning paper and see a disturbingly huge drop in one of your investments on the stock exchange. The numbers don't immediately make sense but in order to comfort yourself you decide to calculate the potential damage, looking over your shoulder you see your phone lying on your bed and now it's a handy calculator.

In a matter of twenty-four hours you have seen your cell phone as three different versions – phone, alarm clock and calculator. In reality the device is still a cell phone but depending on your need it can take other forms, mutate if you will. The concept is the same when we perceive reality. Reality is like the phone, it is always there, but depending on our need we can choose a different perspective to get the outcome that we wish for.

How does perspective manifest into reality?

Figure 1: Perspective to reality

The above figure illustrates the power of perspective and how it manifests into reality.

Let me use a quick example to illustrate what the figure above means. Imagine that your mom asks you to wash her car. The day is blisteringly hot, your hands prune easily after exposure to water and your mom didn't even say please.

The perspective you might have from this scenario is that you have to complete this 'CHORE'. Obviously you won't be too excited and therefore your emotion would be that of reluctance. Due to this emotion associated with the task you don't clean the car very well and the result is an unappreciative mother with a half-cleaned car.

Figure 2: Half-cleaned car

Let us change the scenario slightly from the one above and see the difference in result. Again imagine that your mom asks you to wash her car. The day is blisteringly hot but perfect for tanning your white upper thighs, your hands still look like prunes after exposure to water but luckily you have gloves to wear and as you humbly accept the job your mom sincerely thanks you. Now the perspective of this scenario is that you can complete this 'act of kindnesses' for one of the most important people in your life.

This perspective will awaken excitement within you because everyone wants to make the most important person in his life, his mom, happy. This is woman who has loved you every day, even when you were not so lovable, and therefore your emotion would lean towards enthusiasm.

Due to your motivating emotion to complete the task you clean the car exceptionally well and the result is an over-the-moon mother with a spotless car.

Figure 3: Clean car

Both these perspectives are realistic and highly possible and with the right lenses on we can see the reality we want to help us achieve the desired results. The point of the above scenario is to illustrate that our perspective governs the way we feel, how we feel then directs our actions/ behaviours, and our actions determine the results we see in our lives.

The power in understanding this is that we can decide what result we want – a clean car with a happy mother, and then work back from there. We can determine that a certain result (a clean car) requires this action (attentive hard work) which is governed by this emotion (enthusiasm) which can be created using this perspective (an act of kindness for a loved one). Let's dive deeper into the mechanics behind action.

Our perspectives govern what we see and govern the way we feel

Imagine yourself walking into a room filled with people looking at you. You could perceive them to be staring at your clothes and thinking to themselves; "OMG how underdressed is that person!!" How would you feel in that situation?

I'm known as the colour-blind hipster by my family and friends so I can assure you that I have been there all too often and I'm sure you will agree with me that the feeling is far from great. Another perspective that you could choose is to perceive them to be curiously looking at you because you are wearing a distinctive outfit and that they are intrigued by your uniqueness. How would you feel then? Pretty cool, I would think.

Both scenarios are possible as people stare either out of disgust or curiosity, right? How you choose to perceive your situation makes you feel a certain way. If you perceive yourself to be judged by other people you automatically feel insecure, but perceiving people as taking an interest in you makes you feel special. Our perspectives can change the way we see things, and so change the way an environment makes us feel.

The lotto winner and the wheelchair bound

In 2009 an experiment was performed on two complete strangers, Steven and Paul. They were both pretty average guys; both enjoyed the comfort of good stable jobs, close nit families and had various hobbies to keep their work-life balanced.

The reason these two strangers were chosen for the study was that they had both gone through an extreme life-altering experience and psychologists wanted to uncover how one's perspective changes after such a mammoth change in lifestyle. Steven was the lucky winner of the August Lotto and Paul experienced the tragedy of a horrific accident, which left him wheelchair bound.

Their perspectives and happiness levels were tested as soon as the drastic changes occurred and as you would expect

Steven was on top of the world, ready to fly even higher, while Paul was stuck in the depths of despair dreading his day's further. Three months later both Steven and Paul's perspectives and happiness levels were tested and not much had changed.

Steven was still happy playing golf in Spain, cha cha'ing in Argentina and skiing in the Australian Alps... who could blame him for being happy, right? Paul was still devastated by his condition but was at least content with being able to look after himself and didn't seem to dread every day like before.

Regular visits were paid to both men as the perspectives and happiness levels were recorded to analyse the trends. Once they had reached the twelve month mark both men were interviewed and an astonishing result was noticed. Steven and Paul had accepted the big changes as part of their new lives, both had found contentment and reached a similar level of happiness.

This means that a person who had won the Lotto and a person who had his life shattered by a physical disability reached nearly the same level of happiness after twelve months. This indicated that Paul is in actual fact way better off than Steven.

Steven had travelled the world and experienced wonders his dreams couldn't begin to comprehend, so when he returned to his original life in his small town he was bored out of his mind. He had spent most of his fortune gallivanting around the world and had returned home to live comfortably on the rest of his money. "After seeing exactly what the world has to offer, you see how little you have in your own town." – Steven sighed with frustration.

Paul on the other hand had risen from the dumps and sat tall in his seat as he explained how his life is just perfect. When he had first had the accident he feared that he wouldn't be able to look after himself, that he would need constant assistance which left his pride and dignity in tatters. Now he had made everything in his house paraplegic-friendly; "I can still shower, make food and get my kids ready for school, only one thing is different – I appreciate that I can still do all the small things." – Paul humbly commented on his condition.

This story illustrates how our perspective can completely alter our experience of reality. Steven is still far better off in reality with his life yet it was Paul who soared on the happiness scale. There are always different ways to look at a situation, and each perspective places us in a different state of mind.

Our perspective is powerful as it can govern our emotions. Steven and Paul both had a change in perspective of their current reality and it completely changed the way they looked at life. Steven became hard to please and found fault in every situation after returning home from his world travels where he became accustomed to; 'the good life'.

Paul's world was rocked only to lead him to fulfilment and what is really important in life, such as time with family. Our perspective controls the way we feel every minute of the day and we can choose the way we want to feel by choosing which point of view to adopt.

Our perspectives can either motivate action or result in apathy

If I perceive waking up at six am every morning for work as daunting, tiring and a complete waste of my life then I will have near to no motivation to get out of bed. However, if I perceive waking up at six am every morning to go to a job that I am lucky to have as the economic turmoil is hitting our markets badly, I will feel more positive because at least I have a job. There are always multiple perspectives of your reality, the question is which one motivates productive action more?

IMPACTING GABON

My neighbour Ryan, like many of us, had no idea what he wanted to do with his life after school. He had a passion for travel, enjoyed getting himself out of his comfort zone and had a burning desire to help people in need. Ryan combined these three interests and decided to go on a Peace Corps trip with three friends to West Africa.

The four of them arrived in Gabon in 2009 in the midst of the worst drought Gabon had ever seen. The Gabon people lacked even the basics, like water or adequate food. All that they had to eat was a concoction of chickpeas and spinach; *dish al le Gabon* as they called it.

It was one of the worst periods in Gabon's history and at first sight Ryan's three friends panicked; "We must go home now, it is the worst time to be in Gabon right now." Ryan disagreed; "It is the best possible time to be Gabon. What was the reason for coming in the first place? To help people in need, right? Well, these people need us more than anyone so I am staying!"

Two of the three friends were back on the plane before Ryan had finished his argument though his motivation to make a difference inspired the remaining friend to also stay and help fight the drought together. Three months later Ryan and his friend returned with riches in their hearts that no one else could have ever dreamed of.

They survived the cruellest of conditions and made a difference where it was sorely needed. Ryan went on to study agricultural engineering and is now one of the thought leaders in drought prevention in Africa and he gets to live his passion every day while traveling and helping people.

Ryan had seen the same situation as the two friends that jumped ship but with a different perspective. He saw the potential to improve the conditions and reminded himself that the whole reason he was there was to make a difference. I spoke to Ryan after his trip and he said; "We were so lucky to get there when we did. We were able to touch more lives during this devastating time than if we had gone later on."

It is the filter with which we view the world that either turns mole hills into mountains or turns our obstacles into something beneficial so that we can deal with them in the most productive way possible. Ryan saw an obstacle and decided to see the potential in the experience and that motivated his amazing contribution in helping the needy people of Gabon during the plague.

Our perspectives can either motivate us to excel or cause us to retreat.

There is no denying that our results are based on our actions, our actions are based on our emotions and our emotions are decided by the perspective we adopt. Using this knowledge of how our reality is formed empowers us to take our lives into our own hands by choosing the perspective needed to manifest our dreams into reality.

The power in choosing your perspective

I hope by now that you will agree with me that regardless of the situation there are always multiple lenses through which to view reality.

When doing perspective coaching I often use the story of my first break-up, something that we have all likely experienced. My ex-girlfriend and I were telling different stories of the same situation, we saw the same drawing in completely different colours. She broke up with me because she didn't feel valued and respected, which I guess is a great reason to end it.

From my perspective I felt that I was over-doing the value and respect gestures – if you can ever over-do them. I would never let her open a door, not even my car door, for the duration of our relationship. I surprised her with romantic weekends away and placed her upon a pedal stool of perfection. In the end her perspective and my perspective were completely contradictory but does that mean either one of us was wrong or right?

There are no black and whites, only different shades of grey when it comes to matters of the heart. Our perspectives are not based on reality but based on the preconceived notions that we have become accustomed to. My ex expected me to do more than I was doing, or perhaps to do what I was doing in a different way based on how she believes a respectful gentleman would treat his lady. I knew that, according to my values, I was treating her exactly how I wanted to be treated and had nothing but respect for her.

We had different perspectives based on our values and backgrounds and neither one of us was wrong. Our thoughts are not based on fact but rather on the various ways we are able to interpret our reality through our unique filters.

We perceive reality and try make sense of it the best way we know how; as with the cell phone example in the previous section, perceiving it as an alarm clock is technically 'wrong' as its main purpose is to call though when your phone sounds like an alarm clock at six am in the morning it's understandable that someone would see the phone as an alarm clock.

In the end my ex and I went our separate ways and I truly believe neither one of us was wrong, we were just different. We had our own perspectives on the relationship and the break-up and we were entitled to our differing opinions.

We can choose our reality, the cell phone, to take the form that we want it to have in order to serve our need. I could see the break-up from various perspectives, but which one would help me reach my goal of forgiving and forgetting? Remember no thought is truly based on reality, your thoughts are based on your interpretation and therefore changeable. The best part is that you are doing this all the time, you already know how to change your perspective, now it's about choosing the empowering ones.

Let's get practical

Our initial perspective is never written in stone. We can recondition ourselves to adopt a new and helpful perspective to overcome our obstacles and perceive them in a beneficial way. An example can be walking into a very important meeting; like asking your girlfriends father for her hand in marriage, or having to tell your parents that you are failing school... it doesn't matter.

In the face of these critical conversations you most likely go into a frenetic frenzy of imaginary scenarios to prepare for any likely situation. For arguments sake let's take two believable perspectives that you could have when attending the meeting in order to explain the phenomena of choosing a more positive perspective.

Perspective One; you walk into the room where the meeting is held and an unbearable tension hovers over the room like an ominous woodland fog. The other person is obviously suspicious of your motives and their guard is well up. They are standing tall on the fence opposing you and they will never see things your way. It's pretty much useless even trying because they would never understand, right?

Perspective Two; you enter the room and thankfully the person you wish to see is there on time and ready to chat. He obviously respects you because he has kept to their word to meet with you. The meeting begins with polite pleasantries as the 'big moment' (popping the question) begins to naturally play into the conversation. Things are going great and the answer will surely be positive.

Both scenarios are realistic and possible outcomes, would you agree? The difference is not the in the likelihood of which is more probable but in how the differing perspectives effect your mental attitude towards the meeting.

With the first perspective you go into the meeting with preconceived notions of negativity. Your body language will be depicting your fears, doubts and insecurities and this will make the other person feel uneasy. That undisguisable fear you walk in with will make the other person feel uncomfortable.

You might then see this person's discomfort and take it as a sign that what you feared is coming true, that you will be rejected. Due to your focus being on what could go wrong any sign of failure will be picked up by you. Perspective one creates needless worrying, which is using your imagination to create unwanted scenarios.

The second perspective is as likely as the first but empowers you with a positive energy when entering the room. A smooth comfortable smile will adorn your face as you serenely enter the room. This will immediately put the other person at ease and create a synergetic and supportive environment. Your focus will be on what could go right, and as with perspective one, you will be attuned to finding favourable body language to reinforce your imagined scenario of success.

I am not saying that seeing the situation with a different pair of eyes automatically changes it but it does change your mental attitude going into the situation. If your mental attitude is aligned to positive results you will then radiate and attract positive energy and positive results.

"It seems so simple, Laurens" – Everyone always says when I explain the phenomenon of choosing a helpful perspective. I always reply with the same thing; "It is simple, but it's not always easy." After the break-up with my ex many people told me, as I'm sure they have told you before, "just get over it." As if 'letting go' was such an easy thing to do, something that we hadn't considered of before.

The same applies to changing your perspective. It sounds simple and logical but it takes time, effort and practise to realise the benefits of changing your perspective. You have got the ability because you do it with your phone everyday depending on your need... all you need is practise.

Think about the time you got a brand new phone, I'm sure it took you at least a couple of days before you figured out all the buttons, applications and gadgets the phone possessed, but as you practised and got use to the phone it became second nature. You already know how to have different perspectives of the same thing, now you can learn to use it for your benefit.

Perspectives at work

Imagine yourself sitting outside your manager's office. You have been at the company for over two years and you have barely seen an increase. The company is doing reasonable well and there aren't any noticeable red flags deterring you from a decent increase. While sitting outside waiting for the manager, you run through a few scenarios in order to prepare for the meeting.

I'm going to tell you what you already know and that is that the following pep talk is not a helpful boost before a salary negotiation conversation. "What if he fires me for asking too much?" "What if I haven't performed enough?" "Perhaps the company only gives raises after four years?" – All of these leading down the path of discouragement and fear.

This self-talk is 100% under our control and can be altered. Again it might not change the reality, perhaps there is a rule that only after four years you get an increase but at least changing the conversation in your head will enhance your motivation to try.

You could change the script slightly to give yourself the edge on the negotiation, some beneficial perspectives could be;

"He's acknowledged that I have worked hard." "If I don't ask, the answer is no anyway... I have nothing to lose." "He's a reasonable man, and the company is doing well." – Which will at least boost confidence in trying.

Our thoughts are not real, they are based on our own filters and interpretations. We can change them and so change our lives. If we change the way we perceive a situation, we change our behaviour and actions in that situation and so change the outcome. As when turning the ignition in your car, the car won't move until you act and push the accelerator. You can change reality through your actions.

The critical part of this method to changing your life is that you have to stand up to yourself. It is so easy to fall prey to self-defeating conversations... easier to aim low and hit than aim high and miss. It's now time to challenge yourself, challenge the status quo.

Challenging the status quo

Julie, my elder sister, and I decided that a little bonding break was needed. After searching the web for affordable paradise locations, Durban made it to the top of our list. It didn't take much convincing after you saw the pristine white beaches, charismatically placid oceans and beautiful surrounding environments on the pictures to sway our decision.

We arrived and first thing went for a walk on the divine beach front. The inspirationally endless sea view lead us to an evocative conversation about our dreams and aspirations. We began to talk about some of the obstacles she faced in the corporate world.

Julie told me that her manager, Helen, gave work to her colleague and completely ignored my sister. Julie felt really disappointed; "It's obvious that Helen doesn't think I can handle the work." – She sighed. I paused, empathically seeing the hurt in my sister's eyes. I asked her if that was factual, if that was indeed 100% true... I was challenging her thought process.

"Yes Laurens it is, I know she thinks Craig is more capable than me." I asked her; "Is it possible that Helen sees that you are extremely busy already and that Craig is new to the organisation and therefore needs work to get going?" She contemplated this for a second and then reluctantly agreed. "Is it possible that Helen really values you and therefore doesn't want to overload you in fear that you might burn out?"

Again she contemplated and reacted more positively than to the previous question. "Actually Helen always checks how I am doing and makes sure that I'm managing, probably because I bring a lot of value to the table."

Both are realistic perspectives and possible outcomes as discussed in the example of the different ways to see a cell phone. The question I wanted Julie to answer was which is more helpful? Which provides a better self-image to portray the confidence needed to excel in the world?

In summary every situation can be seen from various perspectives and these perspectives can motivate our behaviour in different ways. If Julie kept the perspective that she is not good enough she will constantly feel threatened by Craig and perhaps behave inappropriately, but now with her new perspective she will feel appreciated and needed.

She might also feel more comfortable to give some of her workload to Craig and give herself some space to breathe. Julie chose a more beneficial perspective to help deal with her dilemma, the viewpoint we decide to take is fully our choice.

I hope this introduction has illustrated the fact that your perspectives or point of view on life determine your behaviour which in turn creates your reality. Your perspectives are largely governed by preconceived notions and experiences but you hold the power to change unhelpful perspectives and replace them with ones that help you achieve your goals.

It is our choice which perspective we want to use in our lives.

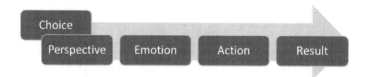

With the power of perspective you can stop waiting until reality is perfect, because you can perceive the perfect reality in the most beneficial way to achieving your dreams.

THE 10 PERSPECTIVE GAME CHANGERS

You cannot control what happens to you, but you can control your attitude towards what happens to you, and in that, you will be mastering change rather than allowing it to master you. As Winston Churchill once said; "Attitude is a little thing that makes a big difference."

Shawn Achor reveals in a TedxTalk, The Happiness Advantage, that a change in perspective can change one's life. The following story is the true story of my upbringing with some of the detail inspired by his talk.

COWBOYS VS INDIANS

When I was nine years old I had a family friend, Clive, who was just six years old. We spent hours playing games together. I was three years older than him which meant that whatever I wanted to do is what we did. I chose to play Cowboys vs Indians.

I immediately ran across the Lego-strewn room and grabbed the broom, which we obviously saw as the gallant stallion, quick to show Clive which side I was on. He retaliated by grabbing a nearby hat, placed his hand over his mouth and began with an Indian cry. Game On.

There are some differing accounts of what happened that day but since my friend is not here with us, let me just tell you the true story, which is that Clive is really clumsy. Somehow without much help Clive inexplicably tripped over my broom, and landed on the ground with a large bang. I looked down, with a devilish smile to see what pain had befallen my poor friend. There he was face down, arms spread and groaning with pain. I was winning!

My devilish delight swiftly turned to a nervous cringe as my parents had charged me with the responsibility of playing safely together, after I had accidently broken Clive's glasses just six weeks prior – fearlessly tackling him out of the way of an on-coming imaginary taxi driver. Clive's face began to pout, tears in his eyes and determination in his demeanour to get me into trouble.

My parents were in the room next door having a sweet summer's day nap, from which they would be angrily awoken. My hysterical nine year old brain went into a frenzy of ideas on how to save my sweet little bottom from red devastation. I turned to my friend and said; "Wait Clive, don't cry, don't cry. Did you see how you landed there, no human being lands like that? Clive you know what that means... that means you could be an aeroplane."

You could see on poor Clive's manipulated face an overwhelming display of conflict. On the one hand his brain desperately attempted to express the pain of being tripped by the older bully and on the other hand he was contemplating his new found identity as a military jet. Instead of a waterfall of tears, angry parents and bottoms flaring with anguish – an uncontrollable smile caressed his face as he took off with all the steam and determination of a fighter pilot.

The rest of the day was spent with laughs, take-offs and happiness as we focused on the fun and the possible, not on the mistake that could've ruined the day. Clive took a different perspective on his situation and made himself feel better.

Bad things are going to happen in our lives, there's no way getting around it. The secret in moving forward happily is determined by the way we choose to interpret our reality. The following subchapters are some of the perspective changers that I have found particularly useful on my journey of fulfilment and internal happiness. Some of the subchapters have a small exercise to help internalise the perspective so that you can begin to choose your own reality.

The ten perspective changers defined in this book are as follows:

1. See every challenge as an opportunity
2. Put yourself in their shoes
3. Long term view
4. Attitude of gratitude
5. It's possible paradigm
6. The art of comparison
7. Everything happens for a reason
8. Circle of influence
9. Impossible to please everyone
10. Facing the fear with belief

1. SEE EVERY CHALLENGE AS AN OPPORTUNITY

Imagine yourself in the following scenario. You have mastered the art of selling a cell phone and have shown record numbers year after year. This leads to your promotion as sales director, providing you with an office overlooking the striking natural scenery, a secretary at your fingertips, not to mention a massive upsurge in salary... things are going your way. Not everyone else is as lucky as you.

Many people have been retrenched due to the economic turmoil and the shareholders are filled with fear for the ever changing stability of the economy. The shareholders are constantly pushing for cost rationalisation and increased financial security.

Your CEO decides that the only way to combat the financial stress at the moment is to grow the market share of the company by moving into a developing country. It had been determined that not many cell phone providers have targeted Sudan as a potential business investment. You being the lead salesman, who is able to sell poverty to the rich, is obviously seen as the go-to man to make this move into Sudan a success. Your confidence is soaring and your eagerness to board the plane to Africa affirms the CEO's decision to send you.

Your arrival at the scenic destination of Sudan is not quite as you expected. On leaving the aircraft you see twenty men standing around the airport holding what seems to be AK47's. Sudan is facing turmoil of all kinds, not just economic downturn. Your concentration, though distracted by the guns at first, focuses back on the problem at hand. Your mind is programmed to see any and every opportunity in sight.

While traversing through the airport you are constantly on the look-out for competing cell phone brands... to your surprise, you see nothing. Your first observation is diligently recorded in your notepad. Sudan market: Point one, no cell phone brands allowed in the airport.

After an hour of customs and illegal searches through your baggage they finally let you go. Leaving the cool and comfortable air-conditioned airport you are confronted by a heat unknown in your home town. You quickly call a taxi mainly to get to your hotel but also because the taxi is the only salvation from the unbearable heat. The taxi driver politely starts a conversation; "Hello sir. Are you here for business or pleasure?" The level of his English is quite remarkable you think quietly to yourself; "Uhm... business." "That's nice, what business are you in sir?" – He asks. "The cell phone business." – You confidently reply. "Cell phone, is that a kind of food?" – He asks inquisitively.

You briefly laugh as you find the question utterly ridiculous but the awkward silence that follows assures you that he has no idea what you are talking about. "Well, you know, like a phone; Blackberry, Nokia, iPhone... Have you never heard of these things?" – You enquire attentively. "No sir, we have nothing like that here." Your first thought is 'What a clueless taxi driver, he doesn't even know what a cell phone is'.

You mind begins to play with the thought and you realise he is extremely well spoken, most likely educated and has a job in a country where jobs are luxuries. If anyone would have a phone he surely would. Your heart sinks as this was not the market you were expecting. Do you see this a challenge or an opportunity?

SHOES IN ARGENTINA

This made up scenario is similar to a well-known tale used by many inspirational speakers in an attempt to inspire a mind-shift change. Two young salesmen had achieved record sales at their shoe company for three consecutive years in a row.

With the need for expansion these two young bucks were sent to an undeveloped area in Argentina. On arrival in the beautiful, nature-dominated town the sales men saw that no one was wearing shoes. Both sales man rushed to their respected rooms and contacted their manager with the news.

The first salesmen's conversation went as follows; "Peter what the hell were you thinking sending us here? There is no market for selling shoes, they don't even wear shoes here." The second salesman saw the exact same reality as salesman one but with a twist and his conversation went as follows; "Wow Peter, thank you for the opportunity. The market is massive, none of them have shoes yet." Similar to the imaginary scenario described above, we can see our problems from different perspectives which could motivate action or dispel desire to try.

I'm not saying that one can view everything as an opportunity but everyone can make the conscious effort to perceive his obstacles as surmountable so that they can deal with them in the most productive way possible. The thing is that everyone faces hardships and challenges throughout their lives. Donald Trump experienced four bankruptcies in a row before making a fortune that no one else could ever have imagined.

The difference between success and failure is the way people deal with hardships. Successful people focus on lessons and opportunities to try a see the problem from a different angle which prompts creativity in finding alternative ways of doing something. Steve Jobs had a different way of looking at computers. He saw that the visual design of a PC was missing and that there was a market for eloquently designed devices. Look at how the world was taken by storm by his genius, by his way of perceiving things from a different angle.

Maybe it's a blessing to be embraced with a challenge as it forces creativity from us and creativity is the cornerstone of success. Often we see similar products absorbing or losing market share due to lack of creativity. Let's take the nutrient giants USN and Herbalife in the South African market for example. USN had dominated for an extended period of time, outselling others as the household product.

Herbalife came into a near saturated market and resided to become a major player through a bit of creative marketing. USN promoted protein enhancement which was obviously criticised from a health perspective, whereas Herbalife came into the market selling the protein advantages but with the added benefit of natural ingredients which eased the doubt of using unhealthy processed products.

Every challenge is merely an opportunity in disguise. Look for an opportunity to grow and you will always find one. Even in the midst of dire disaster if you look hard enough you will always be able to find a lesson.

THE PRO-AM

What did you learn from your last mistake? Raphl Nader once said "Your last mistake is your best teacher" Does this ring true for you?

After my four years at University I decided to join the corporate world. I was lucky enough to be accepted into a Global Company's esteemed Graduate Programme. Four weeks after our introduction into the company we were invited to the most prestigious client weekend event, the Pro-Am.

We were each allocated a mentor/buddy to look after us for the weekend and help introduce us to the various valued clients. On the first night I eagerly approached my mentor and said "Hi my name is Laurens, thank you for your time. I am really looking forward to getting to know you!" His response was "Hey Laurens, my name is Trent, here is your first Tequila shot. We're going to play a game, every time I introduce you to someone you have a tequila shot with them." I replied with "Ah, I know that game, it's called ALCOHOLISM!"

283 awkward introductions later, and I was WASTED. Do you remember the first time you walked into a club? It was the first time partying with your friends, dressed to the nines, the alcohol was flowing, the jokes going and then your favourite song started playing.

You immediately raced to the dance floor and started breaking down with those cheesy Michael Jackson moves, you looked around and it seemed like every girl wanted you and every guy wanted to be you... feeling on top of the world. When in actual fact you were drunk, completely out of rhythm and very unaware of how ridiculous you actually looked. No girl wanted you and no guy wanted to be you. Well that was me in the middle of the dance floor, surrounded by all the clients and executives. That was my first mistake.

Laurens Boel

Next I looked across the room and saw a pretty girl. Now most people at a business function would instantly assume that a young girl is a high-status client's daughter... ah but not me, I break the rules. I approached her with the blue magnum walk, said a word or two and pulled in for the kiss. Now kissing isn't illegal but you see the way I kissed her wasn't the conservative kiss that you would give your grandmother after having tea at her house.

It was more like we had been stranded in a desert for two days without food and water and saw in each other a happy meal. We latched on to each other and began to devour. Before passing out I looked up and saw the CEO of the company looking at me, and that's when my mind said 'Ah I've already gotten this far – why not just completely screw up any chance of career progression?' and my hips began to move, body soon followed and then lastly my tongue joined the party all while facing the CEO.

I woke up on Saturday morning and let me tell you that Hangover 1, 2 and 3 had nothing on how I felt that morning. The graduates wasted no time in telling me I had screwed up my entire career and that I best not go to the function tonight. I was down, out and dreading the next night faced with imminent disapproval from the clients and the company employees alike. One of the sales managers, also a close friend of mine, Manesh, saw I was down and asked what had happened.

I told him the story and a devilish smile crossed his face, he courageously controlled his laughter. He said to me; "It's ok. You've made a mistake but now you have the opportunity to make it right. Everyone is expecting you to fail tonight... prove them WRONG." I was so motivated by his inspiring words resonating through my head the entire night and I was able to re-write the script.

I said no to alcohol – you can by the way, they don't teach you that at school, but you can say no to alcohol. I had a dance off with Trevor Noah who was the entertainment for the night and ended up having good clean fun and adding value to the party. The next day Manesh said to me; "You showed them! You see a mistake is not the end, it just lets you know that you need to tweak your strategy."

It's ok to make mistakes, as long as we learn from them and there is always a lesson within a mistake. Fearing mistakes is to fear trying something new, learning something new. Colonel Sanders, the inventor of the amazing KFC recipe, approached various fast food chicken stores in an attempt to sell his recipe. He endured over a 1000 rejections and only after his 1009th attempt did one store agree to sell his recipe. He got rejected time and time again, he was told he wasn't good enough, his product wasn't good enough. Look at KFC now.

Successful people do what those who fail won't, they try, they fail, they learn and they try again. It's ok to make some mistakes because LIFE doesn't come with instructions, does it? Every challenge contains an opportunity to excel, overcome obstacles or learn valuable lessons.

[See exercises for this chapter at the end of the book]

2. Put yourself in their shoes

How could we understand someone else's point of view? And is it fair to look at life from other's perspective? Navid Negahban challenged many people when he said "You just need to put yourself in someone else's shoes and then see how they feel and then you will understand why they are reacting or why they are behaving the way that they are behaving. We need to be fair."

Putting yourself in another person's shoes is, like Navid said, a fair scenario. As easy as it is to argue that we are always right, every person is entitled to his own opinion and not everyone will always think the way that you do. To put another person's shoes on is not to admit defeat but rather to see the entire game for what it is.

You won't buy a computer just on the basis of physically seeing it, would you? You would have to switch it on, make sure the power supply is correct and that there are no dire defects that you can detect. You need to see the entire picture in order to make a decision.

When putting on someone else's shoes you immediately broaden your horizon to see a bigger and clearer picture. You will almost always see something that you didn't see before that could change your mind-set towards the situation. This is the goal, changing the way you think about something which affects your mood. Change the game so that it works for you, not against you.

VALENTINE'S DAY SURPRISE

A swift love-infused atmosphere filled the air as Valentine's rolled its way into the picture. Our grade four class got into the swing of the magical day by covering the classroom with what seemed to be Cupid's vomit. I was only ten at the time and Valentine's for the boys didn't mean much about love but more about gifts, roses and cute hand-written notes.

Due to my single status I had no interest in getting anyone a special love gift, though I thought I could get a nice friendly gift for my close friend Chloe. I saw Chloe standing in front of our class and I eagerly approached her. Once in her presence she looked at me with a gentle demeanour, hugged me tightly and said; "Happy Valentine's Day Laurens."

Chloe was beautiful, fun, smart and best of all a good friend of mine. Just before going into class I brought my hand from behind my back, containing the special gift that I had bought her. Her eyes widened as she saw the gift and she seemed really excited. Looking back now I truly believe that Chloe was and is a sweet girl because no one else would have faked excitement for that Valentine's gift.

What I handed to her still makes me cringe, a guava juice. My logic was simple, I had no time before school to get her anything but during break I had some small change and saw an almost red coloured guava juice; "Close enough." – I assured myself.

Chloe thoroughly appreciated the thoughtful yet unconventional gift that I had given her, as she began to show it off to her friends. Her friends seemed a bit concerned that I had given her a gift seeing that she had recently gotten into a relationship with a friend of mine, Renaldo. Word spread like wildfire that Laurens had bought Chloe a special *LOOOOOOOVE* gift.

Of course I didn't mean it in a *love* kind of way... for me it was a friendship gift but of course the young kids didn't understand but rather resorted to singing; "Laurens and

Chloe sitting in a tree, K-I-S-S-I-N-G..." Regardless of their constant banter, she and I knew that I had bought her the gift because I valued our friendship.

I saw Renaldo in the distance, across the playground angrily stomping his way towards me... it didn't seem like he saw my gift in a friendship way. As he got near he began furiously shouting; "What the hell man, why did you buy my girlfriend a Valentine's gift?!" I was taken aback by his forceful tone and reacted in much the same way.

A brisk pushing fight ensued but was shortly over with our backs turned and angrily walking in opposite directions. We were both massive pansies so that slight shoving match was all that we could really handle at that stage. The day ended the same way as the rest of the year ensued; a friendship turned sour because of a girl. The only communication Renaldo and I had were short, aggressive and hurtful remarks hurled back and forth.

This really put a damper on the friendship circle as Renaldo and I formed part of the sexy six at school, the nickname we had gave ourselves obviously. There was a spilt within the group and each person was upset with both of us for enduring this petty fight.

The following year I went to Woodhill College and Renaldo and I weren't to see each other for over two years. When we did finally see each other two years later it was much better, there was still a hint of awkwardness but we both knew the petty fight was not worth the drama.

Looking back now I still don't think that what I did was wrong. Chloe was a great friend and the gift represented a friendship that I thoroughly enjoyed and appreciated. That being said if I had just looked at it from his perspective – trying to understand that, even though my intention wasn't malicious, I would have also been upset if someone did the same to me.

With that perspective it would have been much easier for me to apologise. Re-enacting the situation from Reno's side I realised that I would have reacted in the exact same way as him. The commonality would've helped me relate to Renaldo, made it easier to apologise and led to a healthy beneficial relationship.

Sometimes we can't see the entire picture through the mist of one lens and we misunderstand other people. If you try put yourself into the shoes of someone else for a brief moment you would be surprised how differently you view the disagreement.

Remember the last fight that you had with one of your loved ones. If you look at that disagreement from the point of view of the other person how differently does the situation seem?

THE INSATIABLE IPHONE INGESTION

During 2014 I was playing around with the concept of the 4 hour work week which essentially explains how you can work from home and get all your work done in an hour a day so that you can spend the rest of the time doing what you want.

I had great success with the concept and ended up traveling, during working time, with a close friend of mine, Karen. I invited her as soon as I was able to book the trip, with my boss's consent of course, and she was ecstatic. "Of course I'll come."

Two days before she was expected to come over she phoned me tear-stricken; "Laurens, I can't come anymore. My mom didn't pay for my ticket and now doesn't want to pay it anymore." She had a destructive relationship with her mom and a part of me was expecting the cancellation. I didn't really take it to heart.

Three hours later she phoned me back with glee in her voice again. "I was able to loan money for the ticket from a friend of mine." A smile caressed my face as I began to contemplate all the funs things that we would be able to do.

On arrival at George airport Karen looked bewildered and thrilled at the same time. The smell of the sea enticed her nose while the beautiful landscape absorbed her every glance. She saw my mom standing at the arrival desk as I was playing golf and couldn't fetch her.

After a distressingly awful golf game I arrived home to find Karen and my mom arriving in our quaint white Polo. The disappointment of the game was instantly dispelled and my excitement grew. "Thank you for making a plan to get here." – I praised.

Our seven day adventure had just began. The first day was filled with sightseeing, oh's and ah's as the immaculate endless sea view was something she had only experienced in movie theatres. The next few days were spent at the beach, look out points and enjoying a couple of tanning sessions. After the fourth day, like all people do who spend plenty of time together, we began to take each other for granted.

I noticed a constant trend that she would need to look at her phone every two minutes. I became irritated with that, it seemed that social media was more important than spending time with me. Instead of enjoying the view, engaging in conversations or pleasant silence she needed to chat over Facebook, snap chat, Instagram... at times I didn't even think she knew I had left the room. I became quite short with her and tried spending a little more time on my own so that I wouldn't visually show my anger.

On a sunny Friday morning we decided to head down to the whale deck to do some sightseeing and again the phone came with. I decided to take my yoga mat with so that when she began to idly obsess over her phone I could at least entertain myself. I began my usual yoga routine and as always self-reflection was activated. I remember being quite tense due to the frustrations of the robot-like Karen wondering aimlessly around me glued to her phone.

After I turned around and faced the glittering beauty of the endless sea I thought to myself, 'Why am I putting myself through discomfort? Ok, maybe Karen was a little rude being on her phone the whole time but why should I suffer? I am at the sea and should be able to enjoy myself without the need of others constantly entertaining me.'

I used some of the tools I had developed in dealing with anger and the most effective one was to view the situation from her perspective.

She had just gone through a break-up of a one and a half year relationship. Now in any good relationship there are at least five conversations happening per day during the relationship. As soon as the relationship is over those five conversations instantly disappear. I remember when I went through my break-up that I was constantly on my phone, trying to get instant reassurance from the people on the other side of the display.

When I looked at it that way it made it a lot easier to deal with as I was not focusing on how rude it was for her to be on her phone the whole time. I was able to relate to her and understand that what she was going through was a normal reaction. I had also been there and all I wanted was for people to understand that the pain of not being 'loved' was tough. Even though random messages shouldn't equal love, that is what made sense to me and it was ok that it makes sense to her as well.

Karen is one of my closet friends and cares very much for me, she would never intend to hurt me so why focus on the pain? If I were to focus on her trying to hurt me then I would be able to find reasons to prove that true... she's on her phone, ignoring me, doesn't appreciate me... but that is not what she is trying to do so why put myself through that pain?

And just like focusing on reasons to hurt I could focus on reasons to be happy. For example, the fact that she went completely out of her way to get money to buy the ticket to get to George. She had to ask a friend to loan her money which just shows the desire she had to spend time with me... amazing.

Karen was one of my most compassionate friends during my break-up, she enjoyed trying things that made me happy and was someone who would never judge my differences. I remember that she even posted a picture of us two on my Facebook page, which I had deviously hoped someone would do and that my ex would see it. She posted that because she knew I needed to feel 'loved' again.

When we put ourselves in the shoes of others we see our problem in a different way. Sometimes that perspective can help alleviate the pain or trigger a thought that we had not previously recognised. Putting Renaldo's shoes on I figured out that I would have reacted in the exact same way regardless of the intention. This allowed me to see the reason for his reaction and understand his point of view.

Putting on other people's shoes enable you to understand why they are acting a certain way, like Karen and her obsessive phone abuse. 90% of the time the person is not trying to hurt you, they are just dealing with their own problems. Seek to understand and the shoes will fit easily.

<u>SEEK TO UNDERSTAND</u>

October 3rd, 2014. We had just passed the budget period of our company's new financial year and the tension was high. Our managers decided that a well-deserved break was in order and they were right. Our amazing office administrator, Aileen, organised a day breakaway to a lodge, Sable Hills. We arrived and were embraced by nature in all the colours of the rainbow, natural and fresh smells and our excitement grew – this was going to be awesome.

All the members of the bigger team were invited. I knew everyone at the party except for one elderly man. I had seen him multiple times at the office but we had never been introduced. He had quite a hard and stern face and I never quite felt comfortable approaching him. The big chief, Derrick, had just arrived and I eagerly approached him to say hello but he was unfortunately talking to the pre-mentioned stranger.

I decided to back off, as the stranger seemed particularly grumpy. I planned to wait until Derrick was alone to make my move. Derrick and a few others decided to head for a boat ride; "perfect opportunity" I thought. I enthusiastically followed Derrick who was a few paces ahead of me. Derrick stepped onto the large pristine boat and I was quick to follow.

Just before I stuck my hand out I saw the stranger sitting to my right, and again he looked irritable as all hell. "Let me just introduce myself and get it over with" – I thought. I quickly asked one of my colleagues standing close by if he knew the strangers name; "Terry." – My colleague said.

I approached Terry with a polite hand out coupled with a genuine smile. "Hi Terry, it's nice to see you again." I immediately turned as I expected him not to know me, obviously as we had never formally met, and because I expected him not to really care about getting to know me.

He stopped me and said; "I'm sorry but I don't think we have formally met. Could I please get your name?" I was totally taken aback as it was without a doubt the most humble introduction I have ever heard. Terry and I spent most of the afternoon getting to know each other and the grumpy old man that I saw in the beginning of the day completely changed into a kind-hearted and soft-spoken gentlemen.

We sometimes see things that aren't really there. I saw an ugly expression on his face but perhaps he was just thinking of something peculiar, or perhaps was reminded of a work argument. After speaking to him, opening the book, I saw a completely different story.

"When you are too busy judging someone you do not have time to understand them." – Mother Teresa.

THE DRUNK

My manager had come into the office at two pm, walked past my desk and greeted me pleasantly whilst smelling like alcohol. I immediately judged him thinking to myself; "What a drunk!" "Who drinks at this time of the day?" And so on and so forth.

My reaction was not unnoticed as my colleagues asked me why I was in such a foul mood. I explained to my close colleague, Candi, that I thought my manager had a drinking problem and I didn't think I could work for someone with those appalling values. Candi listened empathically and thought it was important to challenge my train of thought.

She said; "Do you think he went out drinking with his friends before work?" "Of course yes" – I replied. She nodded her head and asked another question, "Do you think it's possible that his friend was a potential client and perhaps a drink eased an important business discussion?" "I guess that is possible." – I reluctantly agreed.

She ended with one last probing question. "Would it be ok for him to have had a beer while discussing a client's needs and showing how we can solve that need?" "Yes, that is a fair reason to have a beer." – I said.

Candi then looked at me as if to say 'it's possible and even probable' and she was right. I had immediately tapped into my belief system, which is NO DRINKING before work, and that blinded me to the possibility that he had a good reason for drinking.

The same applies in our lives, just because someone doesn't live up to the belief system that we possess does not mean that they are wrong. Rather replace judgement with a curiosity to understand. Candi stepped out of the judgement paradigm and spent some time asking pertinent questions that completely changed the way in which I perceived the situation.

Candi then said; "If we are too busy judging people we will have no time to understand them." This concept resonates with my core values nowadays especially after an incident where I was the black kettle.

CALLING THE KETTLE BLACK

It was a late afternoon in July and I was enjoying some playful games with the kids at the orphanage that I regularly attend, Hearts of Hope, which almost exclusively houses black kids. Zama and Busi were keeping my attention with constant helicopter and 'watch me' requests. I needed a quick break and decided to play *hide and seek* or how I like to call it *hide until you realise I'm not looking for you* which gives me a few minutes to relax, evil, I know.

I sat down and saw a young white girl walked into the garden, "Melanie" – she politely introduced herself. I immediately assumed that her parents were involved with the orphanage and that she was expected to play with the kids while the parents were visiting. For that reason I thought my time and energy would be best served for the actual orphans.

Melanie was on my leg like hair to skin, not leaving my sight for a millisecond. I kept saying to her; "Ok, go play there. I want to give the kids some attention." I repeated this behaviour for three weeks before one of the care givers asked me what issue I had with Melanie; "Did she say something to offend you Laurens?" – They asked. "No of course not, I just want to make sure the kids that need the attention get it." – I responded.

The care giver looked at me curiously and said; "She probably needs it most. Her dad committed suicide and her mother is a drug addict. She has been through things that none of us would wish on our worst enemy." I was devastatingly distraught.

'How could I have been so judgemental?' I thought. Just because she was white I assumed she didn't need attention, that she wasn't actually an orphan. Not once did she ever come across as one of the orphans, and that just shows you how well people can hide their true emotions. I was so busy judging her appearance that it blinded my vision of her feelings and of the total picture.

Judgement is not a terrible thing, please don't get me wrong. Before housing, technology and safety we used our judgement to keep ourselves safe. Whilst walking through the jungles we had to judge every situation as we were not equipped to defend ourselves against predators. Even today when walking down a dark alleyway and seeing four men dressed in trench coats with their hands in their pockets your judgement of 'that might not be the best alleyway to walk down' could save your life.

The challenge in this day and age is to use our judgement beneficially and fairly. When used unfairly we can easily judge someone for whom they are not and then form resilient first impression of that person which prevents from understanding their behaviour.

Again the wise words from Candi have served me well; "If we are too busy judging people we will have no time to understand them." Take the time and curiosity to understand someone before you place that person into a box.

[See exercises for this chapter at the end of the book]

3. LONG TERM VIEW

What was the last mistake that you made in your life? Perhaps it was to be late for work, drop your lunch or even lose your temper with your best friend. Whatever that mistake was, ask yourself in ten years' time would that mistake matter?

A close colleague of my dad's called one late afternoon happily sharing his promotion to Vice President. My dad was so excited he immediately left home to enjoy this moment with Paul, going out with all the boys for a celebratory evening. The next morning I arrived at breakfast and my dad's expression was not of joy and contentment but of despair.

"What's wrong dad, rough night?" – I cheekily asked. My dad replied without a hint of laughter, "No, Paul died yesterday!" "What?" – I shrieked in dismay. "How dad?" "Heart attack." He sighed. "How is that possible? Was he at high risk?" I enquired. "Not at all. He was under forty, never smoked, drank less than occasionally and did strenuous exercise four times per week" – He replied.

This completely threw me off. I knew Paul quite well from the few brief visits to our home. I never once thought that he would die anytime soon. He was a man filled with the energy of living and enjoyed every moment with a smile. The truth is, we never know how long we have left, and it doesn't make sense to let petty little things stop us from living life to the fullest.

If you were to die tomorrow, is what you are worrying about today really worth your time?

THE NOTE

There was a girl that I had a crush on in high school, her name was Deborah. She knew I existed but only in superficial conversations between classes. A mutual friend of ours, Gert, was celebrating his birthday the following Friday and he invited the entire grade.

The party at times felt less like a party and more like maths class, as we had seen the exact same faces a few hours prior. A few brief hello's and how are you's later and it seemed that the stars were finally aligning, Deborah was approaching me and my pulse began to race. She kindly greeted me with a hug as we began a light-hearted conversation.

Everyone at the party was only sixteen, yet there was alcohol flowing like at a college graduation party. Deborah and I weren't interested in the alcoholic fun and used that commonality to start what would be an extremely insightful conversation.

After standing around and chatting for a good fifteen minutes, we retired to the fireplace where things became a lot more intimate. We spoke about families, upbringings, hopes and dreams... I know that's hectic for a couple of sixteen year olds.

I saw Deborah in a new light, she had not had the perfect life that I had imagined, and she had actually come from a very difficult past. She was the most confident and friendly girl in our school yet behind the mask something painful resided.

I didn't feel intimidated by her confidence but connected with her as a human being. The night flew by as Deborah and I spent the entire time chatting and for one of the first times in my life I had felt completely connected with someone.

The following Monday Deborah ran across the hallway to greet me with a genuine loving hug. We chatted again briefly and went our separate ways to class. "The fire must have done something to give me loads of confidence" – I started telling Bradley, "because now I am petrified of talking to Deborah."

Bradley and I began to scheme how I could overcome this fear and it was unanimously decided that I should write her a letter proclaiming my love... yip, we even used the word proclaiming.

After writing the letter my fears returned and nearly paralysed me. I begged Bradley to give Deborah the note... this was borderline primary school antics but that was how crippling my fear was. Deborah, as sweet a girl as she was, couldn't help herself from laughing at the note and looked over at me as if to say *REALLY*. Needless to say nothing romantic happened between Deborah and myself although we remained friends and for a brief moment in time we saw something inside each other that will forever remain a special moment in our lives.

The days after this embarrassing moment I could hardly bare the humiliation at school, turning red with embarrassment every time. I thought my world was coming to an end, everyone had heard about the note and laughed a lot more impolitely at me than Deborah did. Have you ever felt that after screwing up with a nice person that your life will never be the same?

It took well over six months for me to fully get over the embarrassing disaster. I saw Deborah in the hallway walking to class and thought this was the ideal time to apologise for that note. "Hey Deb's, listen man I just wanted to apologise for that note I gave you a while ago. I was just nervous and couldn't get myself to actually talk to you." – I said. She looked at me very confusedly and said; "What note?" After reliving that hilarious experience she clicked and had a quick giggle. "Oh, no worries Laurens. I forgot about that months ago."

That took the wind out of my sails as I had been sitting with the regret and pain for over six months, when she had forgotten about it just two weeks after it happened. I had made this huge deal out of something that wasn't even worth two weeks of my time.

I should have used the long term view; "Ok, I've made a mistake, but will this really matter in a months' time ... in a years' time? Hell no! So why worry about it now." I unnecessarily threw myself into the tumble dryer of remorse, instead of rationalising the size and impact of the problem.

I could have reduced the regret with questions like; is it really life changing? Or is it just two weeks of experiencing a bump in the road? Acting logically will protect you from going through the unnecessary pain.

MICHAEL WHO?

Can you remember the surname of your first girlfriend? My sister, Katherine, went through an excruciatingly difficult break-up. It was her first love and she honestly couldn't picture her life without marrying him. He shattered her heart by leaving her for another girl, someone that she knew quite well in fact. The day Katherine got the phone call was one of the toughest days in my life. She was crying uncontrollably and I had promised myself that one day I would kick that guy's ass.

The entire family was on high alert to help Katherine through this tough time and with our help she began to move on. The day my dad heard about it he empathised like I had never seen before. He had had a tough first break-up and knew how hard moving on could be. I overheard him reassuring my mom who was devastated, that she could not help Katherine feel better by saying; "Don't worry love, in two years' time Katherine won't even remember his last name."

I couldn't quite relate to how my sister felt, though when I went through my toughest break-up my dad's words rang clear in my mind, 'In two years' time you won't even remember her last name.' Again this shows that we create this emotional turmoil ourselves over something that won't last longer than a short while. I know there are certain times when having a long-term view won't relieve the pain but at least it gives us the perspective that we will be fine again someday.

SILENCING ROAD RAGE

The sun pierced my eyelids through the defenceless blinds as I slowly started waking up. I had been up late the night before and was not keen for another day of work. I reluctantly dragged myself out of my bed and shuffled towards the shower like a zombie. Everything felt like a mission, even pushing the toothpaste out of the container seemed like a mammoth task.

I looked at the mirror and the reflection nearly gave me a heart attack. I thought someone was trying to break in... "Who's the old guy in the reflection?" – I asked as my mind slowly put the pieces together. Bags under the eyes can change the look of a person's face, let me tell you.

I quickly left the bathroom to enjoy a good healthy breakfast and break out of my grogginess. Key to ignition and the purr of my Volvo as I revved her up for the morning travel. I began to run through my three goals for the day, building up the positive motivation to ensure it would be yet another good day to have a good day. I reached the parking lot just outside the building where I worked.

Whilst patiently manoeuvring into the right position to occupy the perfect parking spot someone decided to really push me over the edge. He jumped in front of me and stole the parking that I was clearly aiming for. I was absolutely furious. "Who does this guy think he is?" – I shouted. I punched the hooter, waved my left arm frantically and had some choice words for the thief. He didn't even flinch.

The utter nerve of that guy sat with me like a 'bad hair day' mood until I reached the office. I could barely look the security in the eye, let alone my colleagues, fearing that I would take my frustration out on them. My colleagues could see that something was up and my good friend Jean grabbed me by the arm and said; "Time for some coffee."

I whole-heartedly agreed as this would give me a chance to vent about the idiot who had ruined my day. After grabbing the coffee, we headed outside for a quick chat and it wasn't long until the corrupted driver came into the conversation. "I tell you Jean, he was just trying to piss me off today, and it worked."

Jean had a little giggle to himself because he had never before seen me get angry about something like this. I guess it had to do with the lack of sleep but still I was furious. Jean asked me; "Does it really matter?" "Of course it does Jean." – I barked back angrily." "In one year's time is it really going to matter?" – Jean enquired again. "Probably not." – I replied in a confused manner. Where is he going with this I thought?

"Well if it doesn't matter then should it matter now? All you're doing is getting upset and letting him win." – Jean said. I looked at him in amazement, as in twenty seconds he had completely resized the problem from a mountain to a mole hill. If the problem won't matter in a year's time then what's the point of making it a big deal today? All it does is negatively affect your health over something that has limited importance in your life. Is that really worth it?

It's like a rejection from the pretty girl across the bar. It might hurt in the moment but within a short while you won't even remember that person's name or even remember meeting her in a bar. Life is just too short to give some things priority in your life. Use the long-term view to put into perspective the importance of something in your life. If it's not going to matter in a few weeks' time then does it make sense to prioritise feeling terrible about it now?

[See exercises for this chapter at the end of the book]

4. Attitude of gratitude

Have you ever felt that happiness is like a moving goal post, always visible but just somehow just out of reach? The one day it feels like you've got it and the other day it's impossible to find.

THE JUST SOMETHING AND THEN I'LL BE HAPPY LIE

I felt like that for the entire four years of my University experience. My first year was a constant battle of priorities; on the one hand I was desperately devoting time and resources to studying and on the other fearing the terrifying void of lost friends. "If I could *just* pass and keep my friends *then* I would be happy" – I said. Have you ever said the same *'just something and then I'll be happy'* to yourself?

I grew in confidence in my second year around my studies and my 'free time' had been dedicated to growing my friendship circle. "If I could *just* gain a few more friends *then* I would be happy" – I said. Second year was a hit and my circle grew, my studies went well but my ability to attract the ladies left me wanting.

I could creep them out at a bar, I was just not able to get them to reply to my questions, half way there you might say. "If I could *just* get lucky with girls *then* I would be happy" – I said, starting my third year with the empty promises of happiness as if I really believed that this time it would be enough to satisfy me.

My fourth year was an interesting one. I had achieved all the superficial wants from the previous three years but there was still a vacuum of fulfilment... I need a girlfriend, I thought. So again, like a broken record I thought; "If I could *just* have a steady girlfriend *then* I would be happy." My blessings came and goals were reached but, as though destined, my short-lived happiness always waned. I kept looking for a superficial plaster to replace the void of desolation in my heart.

I passed my first year and kept my friends, though I was not happy. In my second year I made more friends, but I was still not happy. In third year the girls began to take an interest, this didn't make me happy either.

By the fourth year I was going out with one of the coolest girls I know, Suz-lize, but I was still unhappy and I ended up destroying that relationship. I was a lost soul traversing an unknown plane... and I needed direction.

I spoke to my happy-go-lucky friend, Johann, and asked "How do you always stay so happy, bro?" He answered; "If you focus on 'that one' thing stopping you from being happy then you can't be happy, but when you focus on all the beauty and blessings you have around you then nothing can stop you from being happy."

What is that one thing keeping you from being happy right now? Can you think of anything that could put a smile on your face? If you can't find something to be grateful for in your life maybe you could compare yourself to someone who has less? Perhaps you will see things as blessings that before were taken for granted.

IRON MAN DERAILED

I have a cousin in Belgium, David, who was once the iron man of his generation. He would cycle forty km to work, complete a physically intensive job and then cycle back forty km's with a smile on his face and pride in his heart. There was nothing that made him happier than the simple life filled with healthy exercise. In 2010 he was at a rock concert enjoying all that concerts have to offer; limitless alcohol, marvellous music and beautiful people... he was in his happy place.

A storm stuck the festival and devastation hit. A lightning bolt struck a nearby oak tree which crashed under the pressure and landed on the frail white tent where David had taken shelter and landed square on top of him. A handful of people were injured, one or two died and my poor cousin David experienced both; physically injured, mentally and emotionally dead. He is now paralysed from the neck down and will never life his passion of being fit and healthy again.

Every day I get out of bed and walk around, something that he can only dream of doing, and yet I complain more than I rejoice. We walk around every day, and take it for granted where so many people, like David, would give anything to live half the life that we live. Think about someone less privileged than you, what does your life look like compared to theirs?

I asked myself this question and used David as the less privileged person. I looked at my life with bountiful eyes. I looked past the superficial possessions and concentrated on the small things I took for granted that David couldn't do any more like; get out of bed, get food, go for a swim, stroll on the beach or just to wash myself.

All of these humble blessings I had been waking up to daily, forgetting to appreciate them. It was a tough realisation for me, I had to come to terms that I was standing in the way of my happiness. The more I got in life the more I took for granted. In simple terms happiness would be an ever elusive goal if self-satisfaction was not possible.

No material possessions can provide us with sustained happiness. We can see proof of this statement by looking at celebrities. Money is never a consideration for them yet how many are going through divorces, rehabs and relapses in their pursuit of happiness? Getting more is not the answer, the answer lies in how you perceive your surroundings.

I love to use David as my motivation to make every day a good day. As soon as I wake up and remind myself that just getting out of bed is a miracle everything after that is just another blessing. The fact that we have food in our stomachs and a place to call home makes us more blessed than 80% of the world's population. We are blessed and highly favoured.

[See exercises for this chapter at the end of the book]

5. Its possible paradigm

Nelson Mandela had many wise sayings during his immaculate life but this one still rings truest to me, "It always seems impossible until it's done." Do you agree with what he once famously said?

Mandela, with the help of many other influential people, was able to break the ominous chains of oppression of the Apartheid Regime that limited the lives of millions of black families in South Africa.

What he and his fellow leaders achieved would have seemed impossible to absolutely anyone, yet in 1994 the handcuffs of South African slavery were unlocked, and a nation was given its freedom.

During Nelson Mandela's protest of Apartheid he was sentenced to the infamous Robin Island prison for treason. He remained in prison for over twenty-seven years. What is amazing about the twenty-seven years that he spent in prison was that he could have easily opted out of fighting the Apartheid Government and they would have released him. Instead Mandela stuck it out believing that it was possible to end Apartheid and that this sacrifice would achieve his dream.

Nelson Mandela's ultimate sacrifice for his people was enough to inspire other oppressed South Africans to continue fighting. After the twenty-seven year struggle, Nelson Mandela was released to the negotiations that ultimately resulted in the banishment of Apartheid.

Do you think that if for twenty-seven years you stuck to your guns, believing that your dream was possible, never giving up, that you would reach your goal? I have no doubt that it's possible. Twenty-seven years of constantly working on your dream, learning the market, growing yourself, improving your product, reviewing you dream every day and saying to yourself ITS POSSIBLE. Nothing can stop that.

The problem is that we don't see results within a couple of months and immediately we go to the comfort zone of 'it's impossible' and the mind refuses to work on a task that cannot be completed. We finally sacrifice all the motivation to continue with the belief that it is impossible.

Every day we are reminded of people who went above and beyond the perceived belief of "it's impossible". Mahatma Ghandi, Sir Martin Luther King Jr., Mother Theresa, Albert Einstein, Thomas Edison... the list goes on and on.

All of these people were born normal babies, they were not born great they GREW into greatness. They all had a belief that they could make the world a better place and sacrificed their lives, believing that it was possible.

Think about a moment in your life infused with pride because you achieved something amazing. It could be the day you got your degree, bought your first house, got a big shining promotion or even won the hot dog eating competition.

Did it seem possible when you first had the dream? When you first thought of studying Accounting, buying the million Rand house, getting 200% more on your salary or eating fifty hot dogs in a row? Probably not, though as you completed your first year of studying, saved R20 000, got a 20% increase or ate three hotdogs the goal became more achievable. Action is the cure to the impossible curse.

My crippling fear of approaching woman made my goal of attracting an awesome girl into my life a near impossible feat. Through years of trial and error at varsity I finally didn't sweat, cry and eat my words when in the midst of a woman's presence though this still didn't get me a girlfriend. I was a little disappointed that my hard work hadn't paid off yet but I didn't lose hope.

I would constantly look around me and see my friends meeting amazing girls and enjoying fulfilling relationships. Every time I saw a happy couple I would say to myself "If they can find it then surely I will find it too." I hadn't even had a date planned but I knew that it was possible and that kept me motivated to keep my head up and my heart strong.

My girlfriend goal became less of a priority at the start of my fourth year, I really needed to buckle down and get to studying, ensuring woman were not at all on the agenda. It was as if Murphy had planned it out this way that as soon as my time for a girlfriend neared zero he would arrange that I met my first girlfriend. She was and will forever be an absolute treasure in my memory and I am privileged to have called her my girlfriend.

I honestly didn't plan for it to happen, I knew it was possible but I gave up trying to figure out when and how it would happen. It was believing in the possible that kept my motivation up to continuously work on myself, grow into the person who had confidence and ensure that I attracted an amazing girl into my life.

RUNNING BEYOND THE IMPOSSIBLE

Before April 1954 it was deemed impossible for anyone to run a mile in under four minutes. The world had just accepted that it could not be done; "We have reached our physical limit." "We can't go faster." Scientists even did studies on multiple athletes and concluded that it was indeed physically impossible to run a mile under four minutes.

A runner, Roger Banister, shunned the disbelief of the world and took on the challenge. He practised every day with determination in his mind and belief that it was possible in his heart. In the Common Wealth Games of 1954 he ran a mile in 3 minutes 59.45 seconds.

The world sat in silence as Roger transcended to a state that can only be described as marvellous. His belief that it was possible fuelled his fire and made achievement inevitable.

The funny thing about this story is that since Roger ran a mile in under four minutes over 20 000 other people have done it, even high school kids. Have we become bigger, stronger and faster since 1954? I don't think so, people just began to believe it is possible. Roger said in an after-race interview "Just because everyone around you believes it not to be possible, does not make it so."

Roger was competing alone in his pursuit to run the mile in under four minutes. No other runner trained for an under four minute run and therefore there was no competition. If you are insecure about your dreams guess what, everyone else is too. Few people believe that their dreams are reachable and therefore most people aim for mediocre goals.

In Tim Ferriss's book, The 4 hour work week, he describes that over 95% of people believe in setting mediocre goals therefore competition is fiercest for the mediocre. The disbelief of others should ignite determination in you because the competition in reaching that goal will be so slim. You are guaranteed impossible results if you believe it to be possible.

The first step in man's adventure of flight, exploration of the deep sea and travels to the moon began with the belief that it was possible. Great things happen only to those who belief it is achievable. We are constantly reminded of people who achieved the seemingly impossible; Nelson Mandela, Roger Bannister... and if they can do it, why can't you do it too?

OPERATE OUT OF YOUR DREAMS, NOT MEMORY

Les Brown, aka Mamie Brown's baby boy, is one of the world's most renowned inspirational speakers. He started his life on what most people would consider the back foot. He and his twin brother Wesley were abandoned at birth on the floor of a hotel in Miami, USA.

He was plagued at school with the label of mentally educable retarded and was deemed to failure by his teachers and classmates. The constant negative environments in his upbringing were not conducive to learning and growth but rather to a life of drugs and crime.

He failed to get a college degree and had hopes to change the world without the ability to change his own life. This was a man who had no jump start, or platform to spring from to achieve his dream but look at him now. He has multiple business, presents keynotes at most of the Fortune 500 Companies and is recognised as one of the most inspirational people in the world.

I was at the National Achiever's Congress in mid July 2014 where Les Brown was the main speaker. After he explained the heart wrenching hardships that he had faced he roused up the audience by saying;

"It was more than a longshot for me to get to where I am today, it was a miracle, ladies and gentleman. I needed to ignore that inner conversation that was telling me *'it's not possible'*. I needed to ignore what the people around me were telling me that *'it's not possible'*. Instead I looked within myself and found that I'm blessed and highly favoured. It is possible for me to bring my own greatness into this world. 'IT IS POSSIBLE'." The audience rose as Les ended his climatic presentation with; "Operate out of your dreams, not your memory."

Believe that it is possible and work towards it, without worrying about how it comes to pass. If we have the courage to believe that it is possible the universe will provide us the way to achieving it.

20 000 FOLLOWERS

In March of 2014 I had a dream. A dream that everyone around me considered impossible. I wanted to grow my Facebook page followers from 214, of which 200 were friends and family, to over 20 000 by November 2014. I knew my page had a positive message that could hopefully inspire someone, and that maybe I could help a stranger strive to become great.

I was so excited about this dream and I began to tell everyone around me including my family. Every passionate point I made when describing my dream was briskly returned with a destructive reaction. No one could see my dream for me, no one could even say *maybe it's possible*.

Telling my friends produced a lot of laughter and telling my family caused them to worry about my sanity. At the beginning of my inspirational speaking journey my dad didn't think much of it and rationalised it to be just another phase. Though when he heard about the November goal he began to panic, realising that I was putting more energy than expected into my dream. He reacted without thinking, completely out of fear; "What the hell are you doing, Laurens? Stop with this pie in the sky dream that you will never achieve." – He said.

I could handle the banter of my friends without becoming discouraged but after being confronted with my family's doubt of me, my dream slowly faded as the belief of the possibility dwindled to near extinction. Losing the belief that my goal was possible completely stunted my action. I thought to myself "it will be such a waste of time to try because there is no point. I'm doomed to failure."

My dream of inspirational speaking took a slight detour. I closed my Facebook page and decided that my time was better spent elsewhere... I was clearly not going to inspire anyone. Two weeks after the Facebook page had been buried I received a message on my page.

I was completely confused as I thought the page interaction had completely stopped. I reluctantly opened the page again, seeing my wasted efforts displayed on the high density screen and the message read as follows;

"Where have you gone, Laurens? Why have you stopped posting these positive messages?" I re-read that message countless times to determine if perhaps the person sent the mail to the wrong Facebook page. I replied with a sincere apology and explained that I can't inspire people. The instant reply to my apology was: "You inspired me."

A fire, that had been temporarily tamed, began to burn in my heart. "That's RIGHT!" – I said confidently to myself. I am able to inspire people, I am the one who is able to do this and it's possible for me to reach more people. I have inspired this gentlemen and there are plenty of people out there that would also find value in these quotes. I can make a difference, it's possible.

I kept repeating these confidence boosting sentences to myself over and over again. All of them were saying the same thing; 'IT'S POSSIBLE'. I reactivated my page and again fully engaged with my audience. An ominous cloud of worry and disbelief constantly shone from my parents but I couldn't let that dim the possibility any longer.

I found so much inspiration in that one message and it made me realise that reminding myself that 'it is possible' is the coal with which the fire of determination is stoked. Whenever I am faced with the menacing doubt of impossibility I put on the Les Brown's YouTube presentation, *It's Not Over Until I Win'* – which to this day is my favourite thirty minute keynotes of all time.

The presentation is filled with amazing points of inspiration but my favourite is when he speaks about his dream of becoming an inspirational speaker and everyone around him laughed. They said you have no degree, no corporate experience and you're not worth aspiring to... why would anyone ever listen to you?

Les pauses to allow the statement to be absorbed and continues; "It's hard, ladies and gentlemen. The thing about your dream is that even when others don't see it for me, I MUST see it for myself!" – Les powerfully belts out.

[See exercises for this chapter at the end of the book]

6. The art of comparison

17th September 2014, my palms were slowly starting to sweat as my hands forcefully gripped each other, taking turns to squeeze my ever handy stress ball. I was hearing the noise in the office but listening only to the thoughts in my head. It sounded like a broken record player, over and over again the same message "I hope it goes well tonight."

It was the first time that my family and mentors were going to hear me speak. "I hope it goes well tonight." It was our usual 3rd Wednesday of the month Toastmasters meeting and I was frazzled. "Only two more hours until its go time, I can't wait, Laurens." – Candi said. Again the record player reported "I hope it goes well tonight. It has to go well tonight."

Needless to say I was anxious about the meeting. I had also invited my sister, Julie, to join the meeting where she would give her second speech. I thought because my parents are making the fifty kilometre trip all the way from Pretoria they may as well hear Julie speak, regardless of the fact that it was only her second speech.

Julie and I had arranged to meet thirty minutes before the meeting so we could quickly practise our speeches for each other. I met Julie in the parking lot and could see from her body language that she had stressed the entire day about the upcoming meeting.

We gave each other a hug and I could feel the rush of what seemed like three shots of espresso anxieties coming from Julie's embrace. I might have been nervous but Julie was completely freaking out.

We went inside. I quickly showed her what the meeting room looks like and grabbed her a glass of water. Once the tension eased a little, we dropped everything and assumed positions for a quick rehearsal of the speeches. Julie was first up and she spoke beautifully; her body language was comfortable and open, her eyes engaging, her word images were vivid and the confidence she portrayed was that of a veteran speaker. I applauded as the pride in my heart was worn on my sleeve; "Wow Julie, you've upped your game. I am so proud of you." – I praised.

Next up was me to take the stage and perform my speech. The sweat vanished from my palms as the comfort from my sister's presence soothed my doubts. After finishing my last line I looked up and saw my sister's face lighten up as pride touched her smile. "Wow Laurens, you are really becoming an amazing speaker." A quirky and shy smile crossed my face... I was ready for the meeting.

I saw my sister's smile revert back to her usual Monday morning expression. "What's wrong Julie?" – I enquired. She said; "I wish I had heard your speech earlier last week then I could have added some of those amazing body language movements and vocal varieties that you had in your speech. Ag man, mine is so bland right now." I was stunned by her reaction.

She had only said her first speech ever two weeks ago and she was now comparing herself to someone who had been speaking five times a week for over a year and a half. "Julie, it has taken me over eighteen months to be able to naturally add body language and vocal variety to my speeches. It is unfair for you to compare yourself with me." She was losing motivation to try because she wasn't as good as someone who had had over a year more experience than her.

The comparison tool is like a hand gun, it is extremely powerful and when used in the wrong way can be deadly. If someone holds a gun the wrong way round and then shoots you can only imagine what a disaster that would be.

Comparing yourself to someone who is on another level will only make your efforts seem less than what they are, and so chip away at your confidence. On the other hand when a trained officer of the law wields the hand gun, with poised hands, its power can be used to great effect.

Comparing ourselves changes the view of the game, our reality. Take a second and view your life from your mom's perspective. How different a view is that? Imagine what your pet's view is of you, how cool a person are you from his perspective? The point is that we are still the same person but seeing ourselves from other people's point of view give us a different take on life.

This concept is the basis of self-motivation. We can choose a perspective that will motivate the right behaviour in a certain situation. If you are struggling to study and you compare yourself to the likes of Steve Jobs who quit his studies and went on to make millions, you might not feel compelled to study, right?

Though if you compare yourself to someone who didn't have the privilege of going to varsity because his parents couldn't afford it, maybe that would drive more motivation because your parents did everything they could to offer you that opportunity?

CINEMATIC REVELATION

My sisters, Kat and Julie, and I had a craving to go to the cinema together, something we hadn't done in what felt like years. While sifting through the movie options one particular movie stood out above the rest, 'The City of Violence'. This was due to two reasons, one was that we all loved scary movies and it sounded pretty damn scary and the more convincing reason was that the movie had been shot in South Africa.

We eagerly arrived at the cinema, rushed to get some salty popcorn and dashed to our seats. The movie displayed the hardships that are faced in South Africa; crime, gangster pressure, lack of family support and drug abuse. After the movie ended my sisters and I sat in silence for a minute contemplating what our perspective of the movie was. We looked at each other with wide eyes as if to say, 'wow, that was hectic'.

After collecting our thoughts briefly we began in a heated discussion about what we thought the movie's message was. We engaged in a bit of healthy sibling banter, respectfully disagreeing about the scariest scenes and what the ultimate story line was. Once the dust settled on that debate we began to talk about the hardships faced in the movie. How some people don't have a stable upbringing, and some don't even have family to look after them.

Katherine then brought this hardship closer to home by saying; "Almost all of my friends' parents are divorced and they didn't grow up in a stable environment. It doesn't just happen in the movies." This got both Julie and myself to contemplate which of our friends' families are still together. None of my five closest friends' parents are still together; two families had experienced adultery, one family endured severe depression... and all had suffered deep wounds of insecurity.

My sisters and I looked at those families and saw within our family pure gold. Our parents obviously fought and disagreed, but they always made it through the tough times and enjoyed the great ones. Through thick and thin they made it work, they were of the belief that if something was broken they would not throw it away but fix it.

We looked at our lives, about how blessed we were, we never had to worry about parents constantly fighting, broken homes or alcoholic tendencies. That comparison gave us the world of confidence because we realised we have an extremely strong base to work from. We can go through turmoil but you had better believe that my family will be right there, lifting me back up to my feet. This is an example of a positive comparison that changed the way we feel, think and behave in a constructive way.

Sometimes we have these extremely unrealistic expectations, like in the case of Julie's speech, to the point where the determination to continue is overpowered by the fatigue of not improving fast enough. Setting realistic goals is important because as we reach these smaller achievable goals we begin to gain motivation, we begin to believe more is possible and as we progress our goals may become bigger.

My initial dream wasn't to become an inspirational speaker set on changing the world. I started by first inspiring my family in a few meek conversations. I then started a Facebook page to inspire my friends, from there the feedback was great and continued to grow my audience. I joined Toastmasters to inspire people through speaking and from visiting my home club twice a month I went to visiting various other clubs three times a week.

I am grateful to say that I am now inspiring over 30 000 people on a daily basis through my page and I am continuously asked to speak at various Toastmaster events. I didn't start with the seemingly unrealistic 30 000 goal but as my goals were reached I celebrated and began to set bigger ones to eventually reach that significant mark.

Comparing our lives to someone else changes the way we view our lives. It is up to us to choose which comparisons are worth our time. We can compare ourselves to people who are way advanced and took years to get there, ultimately pointing the gun at ourselves or we can compare ourselves to people who faced difficulties we could never imagine and in doing so see the hidden blessings all around us.

It is a powerful tool we can use to drive motivation or destroy determination, and we get to choose who to compare ourselves to and to what extent the comparison is necessary.

MANAGER EXCHANGE

During the end of our financial year at work it felt like I had been pushed overboard with only a life vest to keep me afloat. My manager, Trevor, had suddenly quit for an unknown reason and left me with expectations unmet and plans unfinished. Luckily Trevor's manager flew down from Cape Town to put out the fire of his disappearing act.

I was like an orphaned child as Trevor's manager tried to pawn me off to another team, which fortunately they agreed to. I would join a new team, in a new role, under a new manager named Kerry.

It was four weeks after I had joined the new team and there I was, in the middle of the sea with only a lifejacket to keep me afloat. I had no idea what the expectations of my role were, when my increase was coming or the extent to which I might travel. The only information I was given by Trevor's manager is that I was going to move to America for six months, which was the metaphorical lifejacket keeping my hopes up.

I constantly imagined all the adventures possible in America; from drinking high-speed coffee in New York, to *beaching* on the immaculate Miami Beach front and if time permitted, visiting the infamous Las Vegas.

The possibilities were endless and diminished my fears of the unknown job expectation to some extent, though after four weeks I became irritated and arranged a meeting with Kerry to gain some insights into my role.

Kerry jokingly called me into the office the next Tuesday saying; "Laurens, you're in trouble, come join me in my office." To which I cheekily replied; "Promise. Where is the naughty corner?" I felt very comfortable with Kerry and I was quite excited to work with her regardless of the lack of clarity in my role.

Her initial comment as I closed the door behind me, killed my good mood; "Laurens, I think there might be an unrealistic expectation of your travel plans this year. You won't be able to go to America."

My lifejacket had just been agonisingly torn off my body as I was expected to fend for myself; "Ok" – I said as feelings of disappointment filled within me. I was under the impression that I was moving to America to target the growth we had planned there but those expectations were grossly misunderstood. Kerry kept her composure while spilling the bad news even though I was reacting poorly to the information, frowning and hissing with disapproving remarks.

Kerry had a great way with people and could see this young man had been taken on an unfair trip, led to believe the impossible. She kindly spent the next twenty minutes plotting out the plan for my possible travelling adventures. She really impressed me with her approach, as she took time helping me to understand my travel implications and also try to re-manage the expectations that other people had misplaced.

My old manager, Trevor, was a completely hands-off manager, barely helping me get around, introducing me to people or even coaching me about the product. Trevor left me to my own devices, stranded on an unknown island to fend for myself. At first I was quite disappointed about not going to America, but the way in which Kerry had handled the situation left me smiling gleefully after leaving her office.

I excitedly phoned my family with the good news. I didn't feel the disappointing gloom of not going to America but rather I saw the exciting prospects of the possible travel around the world and experiencing different adventures. After the ecstatic calls I engaged in some self-reflection as I reminisced; "She handled the conversation really well and then again so did I, I wonder why?" – I contemplated.

It became clear to me that although I was disappointed that the travel situation was not as great as I had first anticipated I saw a lot of positives in the new role. Firstly I would still get to travel to some extent, I had an interesting job description and most importantly I had a manager who was hands-on and willing to guide me back to the boat when she saw that the lifejacket wasn't keeping me afloat.

I had a standard idea of how managers manage their employees, set by Trevor's reasonably poor example. I unconsciously used my experience of working for Trevor as a comparison to Kerry, this gave me the comfort that although things haven't panned out perfectly at least I was blessed to have a supportive manager like Kerry. Although Kerry might not be the best manager, because I was comparing her to one of the inferior managers, she seemed to knock the lights out.

This unconscious comparison is what made the transition from disappointment to excitement of the new role so quick and easy. This comparison helped me to leave the office with energy and excitement and also made a great impression with Kerry as if to say I am a team player and I will make the best of any situation.

I hadn't once been aware in the meeting that I was using comparison to help me with this situation but as I reflected I saw that that was the tool that my mind automatically employed. This was a very exciting revelation for me as I began to see the fruits of my efforts, I had finally spent enough time on habitually practising the art of comparison that it became natural for me in changing my perspective to my advantage.

The perspectives in this book require constant practise but as you begin to see the benefits your mind will associate perceiving the world in a certain way with a good feeling. This creates a positive unconscious habit to constantly reframe reality to making it work for you, not against you.

[See exercises for this chapter at the end of the book]

7. EVERYTHING HAPPENS FOR A REASON

> *"I believe that everything happens for a reason. People change so that you can learn to let go, things go wrong so that you can appreciate them when they're right, you believe lies so you eventually learn to trust no one but yourself, and sometimes good things fall apart so better things can fall together." – Marilyn Monroe*

3 YEARS OF HARD KNOCKS

"I'm sorry Laurens but it's over, I want us to see other people." – She said in a serious tone. "What, but why?" – I asked fearing the worst. "I just don't love you anymore." "I will never love again." – I said dramatically as she turned and walked away into the distance.

Ah, don't you enjoy reminiscing about your wretched first break-up? Mine was at the tender age of thirteen where I foolishly thought my life could not get any worse... until puberty hit. I don't know about you, but when everyone heard that my dream girl, certain wife and best girlfriend of two weeks had broken up with me their responses were all the same; "I'm sorry Laurens, but remember everything does happen for a reason, I'm sure it will work out."

And you're left stranded, looking at this person in utter confusion. What the hell am I supposed to do with that knowledge? Everything happens for a reason, what does that even mean, how does that even help?

Do you believe that everything happens for a reason? My first three years of University tested my belief that everything happens for a reason.

In my first year of University my appetite for food increased and in turn my waist began to thicken. The first year spread hit me pretty hard, and my relationship with Nutella was stronger than ever. That's when I decided to join a soccer club, to get rid of the extra jelly. The team needed a defender and that's where I slotted in. Now defending is pretty cool, but have you ever heard of a defender doing a dashing dribble with a finish to boot, scoring the winning goal, and attracting the hottest cheerleader? No, but that was about to change.

I had been practising immensely hard for our last game, and I was determined to score. By the end of normal time the game was tied, three all. Three goals scored by our team and three goals scored by theirs. Well, two goals scored by them and one heroic, swivelling left-foot-bicycle-kick ending in a Zorro pose... own goal by me. I told you I would get my name on the scoreboard, though in all honesty I felt like a complete idiot. The draw obviously meant that we had to go to penalty shoot-outs.

I had let the team down, my frantic nineteen year old brain went into a frenzy of ideas on how to rectify this mistake. I saw how everyone was dreading to take the first penalty. I went up to the coach and begged "Please let me take it, I've made a mistake and need to make it up to them – also I have already scored maybe that's good luck." He replied with silence and a stern-faced expression, signalling that he didn't find the joke very funny.

I walked up to the penalty spot thinking to myself that I really need to dig deep and score this goal... to make it up to the team. I was determined. While walking up to the penalty I was gripped by multiple fears; what if you miss, what if the team loses, what if you fall... I dismissed each fear, repeating to myself, 'I have to do this for the team, I have to make up for the mistake'.

I ran up full speed past all of the fears and doubts and struck the ball powerfully, while keeping my eyes shut. I didn't want to see where the ball landed. There was just silence. I thought to myself, 'How bad was this penalty kick that I don't even deserve a *boo*?' I slowly opened my eyes to a standing ovation from my teammates and a roaring crowd, my mom and dad included, cheering me on.

This goal inspired my teammates into believing that they too can score, especially if the idiot scoring the own goals could do it. My coach grabbed me before I joined in celebration with the rest of the team; "Well done Laurens, you've proved that you can bounce back." My confidence amplified whilst running towards my team... I had made a mistake but maybe the reason was to rise above and make right the wrong.

In my second year I wondered 'Why can't I attract a girlfriend? I have a car, what more do I need?' That was naïve of me. And of course the whole "scoring the own goal" reputation wasn't helping.

In the midst of my dry spell and utter lack of confidence something quite amazing happened. I got a cute look from a pretty girl in the club. I say cute look because I was used to the 'creeped out' look. You see I was the guy who would make eye contact with every girl in the club, until one of them looked back at me.

The staring competition would begin... and I would stare for just that second too long when she begins to think 'Oh dear God, I hope he is looking at the girl right behind me.' So when I saw her genuinely looking at me I jumped at the opportunity.

I faked as much confidence as I thought possible as I approached her with my blue magnum look, when out of nowhere, this chair flies in from the left and tackles me to the ground. I tried to turn my stumble into a dance but everyone around me just thought I was having a seizure. As I looked up, I saw that she was standing right in front of me.

The only part of my game that I had practised was my opening line, the introductory ice breaker. I had planned to say something like; "Hi my name is Laurens, nice to meet you." Short, sweet and to the point. If she replied, I would take it from there. Being that this was the only part of my game that I was confident with, I made sure to do it with self-assurance. I stood up with determination, looked her straight in the eye and said with ultimate conviction; "Hi I'm meet, it's very nice to Laurens you."

What followed was thirty seconds of excruciating silence. "Well now this is awkward" – I said, in an attempt to break the silence. But as we all know that saying that makes things just that much more awkward. She began to turn her back to me. Now, I'm not proud of how I reacted next but you must understand, I was extremely desperate... I jumped to my knees and pleaded "I have a car..."

She and her friends hurriedly left for the dance floor in fear that I would follow them – attracting girls is the easy part, but repelling them to the point where they are scared for their lives, well now that takes a special skill – one that I have acquired.

Everyone in the club was staring at me laughing and pointing, with glares of disapproval. My confidence was shot. I had made a complete fool of myself and was the laughing stock. This was my worst nightmare... because isn't rejection everyone's greatest fear? In the midst of laughter,

113

pain and regret, a group of people, my friends, surrounded me and banished the rejection with reaffirming comments and jokes along the way.

I didn't get the girlfriend I wanted that night, but I did take comfort in knowing my friends will be there for me when I need them. They didn't focus on the rejection or the mistakes I had made... they came to cheer me up because they wanted me to have fun. When I have fun they have fun.

Maybe the reason for that excruciating experience was to value what my friends think of me instead of what the random people that mean nothing in my life think of me. I left the club not hearing the giggles and comments of the people making fun of me, but rather I felt blessed and highly favoured because the right people love me.

In my third year of University, I was still single obviously, and my friend and I decided to start a business together. We borrowed R20 000 from our families to start an online business, and while I don't want to brag, in just six shorts months we took that R20 000 debt and we doubled that debt. That's right we took our e-business idea and turned it into a Non-Profit Organisation.

Our friendship took a huge knock, to the point where we didn't want anything to do with each other anymore. The last thing I ever heard from him was; "Thanks to you the business failed." That was a tough one. I wasn't perfect and I agree I made a lot of mistakes but he was certainly not a diamond in a coal mine.

I wasn't quite sure how to see the life lesson in this situation. I spoke to my mom about what had happened and what she said to me rang so true. "Wow I'm glad he showed you who he really is before the business got bigger. Now you have more space and time in your life for the right people."

Sometimes you do let your team down, be it family, a sport's team or your significant other, but the reason could be that you get the chance to make things right again, to believe that you can make mistakes and it's not the end of the world, it's an opportunity to grow and learn.

Sometimes people make you feel inferior and stupid, but the lesson could be to help you find and focus on those that see the greatness within you. Sometimes you face hardships, be it emotional or financial in order to see the true colours of people around you.

So when faced with a failure, whether it is letting someone down, a rejection or a failed project, look for a reason why it's happened and you will not only find one but it will comfort and grow you into a better person.

LEAVING VICTIM CITY

Imagine yourself walking into your local bank on a lazy Saturday morning. The sun is shining, birds are singing and everyone greets you with a polite smile. As you reach the reception area you are embraced with a kind-hearted; "Welcome, how may I be of service to you on this beautiful day?"

Everything makes sense in the world as you take your rightful place at the back of the line. The thirty people in the bank are seemingly friends as the conversations are quite rowdy. Once you join the line you are engaged into small talk. The delightful discussion is brought to an immediate halt as a gunshot is fired through the roof of the bank.

As you turn around you see that five robbers have rapidly entered the bank, and they are not there to make a deposit. The friendly atmosphere in the bank vanishes as the bank robbers take control of the show. The robbers command everyone to sit down and shut up, which each person does without question.

They begin to alleviate the tellers of the money in their safes, the tension is high and any mishap could push the unstable and scared robbers over the edge. The robbers' patience is worn thin when they hear the sirens of the police brigade approaching the bank. All the bank's customers begin to feel a sense of safety and calm – but not for long. The robbers realise that the police are too close for them to escape and they decided to hold someone hostage.

They grab the least physically fit person, a petite elderly lady with crutches, as she won't have the strength to fight back. This causes alarm bells in the customers' minds and they rise up to fight back. Three large men run towards the robbers in an attempt to protect the elderly lady. The robbers panic when they see the men charging and before being tackled to the ground they fire one menacing bullet.

Everyone frantically looks around to make sure that the bullet didn't kill someone. You also begin to observe the other people in the bank to see if any injuries had befallen them. While scoping the area for a potential victim you realise that all the customers are looking at you empathically.

Your adrenaline-induced fear ceases once the police charge in, taking control of the situation and the pain of being shot in the shoulder pierces your nerve endings. "That is why they were looking at me so strangely" – You say to yourself. Would you see this situation as lucky or unlucky?

In the book 'The Happiness Advantage', Shawn Achor speaks of the test done on multiple individuals describing a similar scenario as above and then asking the question of whether they considered themselves to be lucky or unlucky. Around 50% leant towards being lucky and the other 50% thought they had been unlucky.

The unlucky half said; "The mere fact that I was the only one shot in the entire bank means that I am unlucky," The lucky half had a different perspective on the scenario; "It was lucky that the bullet that hit me was not fatal, and we are also lucky that no one, especially the sweet old lady, got hurt."

The unlucky group of people had seen the scenario as debilitating which caused them to feel like a victim in their story. To what extent does victimising yourself put you at a disadvantage?

THE VICTIM DISADVANTAGE

Again in Shawn Achor's book, 'The Happiness Advantage', a test was done on dogs. The dogs were placed into a controlled closed off area that had a siren within ear shot. Whenever the siren went off the dogs were shocked ever so slightly. The first experiment consisted of the dogs placed inside the closed-off area and every time the siren went off they received a little jolt.

For the next experiment they took the dogs into a slightly larger controlled area that was divided by a small divider. If the dogs were in the one section of the controlled area when the siren went off they would be shocked, but if they went to the other section of the compartment they would not be shocked.

Everyone assumed that the dogs would jump to the next compartment, even though they knew nothing about the experiment, but surprisingly they didn't. They just sat in the one section and experienced the jolts after every siren went off. It was concluded that the dogs were conditioned to feel helpless in the first experiment and therefore had no intention of trying, the *'what's the point, I can't change it'* mentality.

Once this was agreed they did both the experiments on two groups of people; Group one would be conditioned to feel helpless by being subjected to experiment one, followed by experiment two, and Group two would only be exposed to the second experiment.

The scientists assumed that the people from Group one would try alleviate the pain by moving around to the controlled "pain-free" area, yet, just like the dogs, they didn't, they just stood there and accepted the torment as if they deserved it. Interestingly, Group two, who had not been conditioned with the helplessness mentality, tried to alleviate the pain and moved around so that the jolt would not affect them.

The experiment had the same effect on both dogs and humans. It was concluded that the conditioning of helplessness is an extremely powerful impediment. The first group were exposed to physical pain, but not even this pain could inspire action from them, because they believed they couldn't do anything about it and therefore didn't.

If we see ourselves as helpless in our lives, the victim of the day, we will have no motivation to try and change things. Looking for a reason why you are going through the hard times will prevent you from falling prey to victimising yourself. Everyone goes through trauma and hard times, no one can escape it, but we can choose whether we are the victims or the heroes who have grown from the experience.

If we are looking for a reason why something has happened we will most likely find one. Finding one reason why something has happened could be the difference between feeling victimised and taking charge of your life. Don't be the victim, look for a reason why you have been tested and use it to be the powerful hero in your own story.

[See exercises for this chapter at the end of the book]

8. Circle of influence — Accept
WHAT YOU CANNOT CHANGE

If you were to rely on sunny weather in order to have a good day, how much control would you have over your own happiness? If you were to rely on someone else giving you a compliment in order to feel good about yourself, how much control would you have over feeling worthy? If we give the power to someone else or external circumstances to control the way we feel, we have no guarantee of finding happiness.

This same analogy applies to all aspects of your life. If you were to rely on someone else to write your biography for you, how sure would you be that it is factually correct? If your goal is to excel at golf, how much can your coach really teach you if you do not practise? Although you may be in an enabling environment it is up to you to make it happen.

In order to be effective in life we must focus our energy on the things we can control. When we rely on external circumstances to motivate the right feelings or behaviours we may end up waiting indefinitely. If you are faced with a challenge in your life where the outcome you desire is dependent on someone or something else it is imperative that you firstly acknowledge this state of mind and secondly convert your focus and attention to what YOU can do to achieve your goals.

When placing our hopes in someone or something else we have absolutely no control on how it will work out, and if it doesn't work out we cannot fix it. In these instances you should look at the situation from the point of view where you can effect change and measure your success by your actions only.

As you already know – people and situations aren't always going to work out as planned and more often than not we cannot do anything about this. Rather, we need to empower ourselves to overcome the helplessness by changing our focus to the elements of the situation we can control – ourselves.

<u>BIRDS OF A FEATHER</u>

I went to a speaking seminar and had the chance to meet one of my hero's, Les Brown. That weekend seminar took me to a new level of consciousness. The most profound statement that he made was, "It is necessary that you get the losers out of your life if you want to life your dream." It is quite a statement, but it could change your life, right?

As mentioned in previous chapters I lost a close friend of mine, Greg, to drugs. He was a happy-go-lucky, slightly nerdy kind of guy with a heart of gold. When he started spending time with the wrong crowd he was adversely influenced and transformed from a best friend into a masked stranger. I got back into contact with Greg to try help him onto the right path and while speaking to him I was reminded of the power of surrounding myself with quality people.

As we spoke I realised he had become a complete stranger to me, all I saw was a shell of my former friend. He was no longer the person I sang songs with at school to annoy our teachers, it was clear that he had changed and become more like the people he surrounded himself with. His friends and family didn't recognise him anymore nor relate to the person he had become.

This conversation with Greg was a defining moment in my life and taught me that we become like the people we surround ourselves with. From this point forward I have consciously decided that I will only spend time with friends and people who have a positive impact on my life. I would not settle for anything less than the best.

This decision was not without repercussions as during this time of reflection I realised that my best friend at the time was bringing me down and I had to walk away from that friendship. It was extremely tough at first but I soon started benefiting as I my weekends were no longer filled with alcohol and meaningless attempts to hook up with girls, rather I had time to work on my dream, on myself.

Following from this situation with Greg as well as some lessons learnt in my younger, more gullible days, I now had a yearning desire to learn from people and spend my time in growing myself. This mind-set would prove to be hugely valuable in my journey of self-mastery, and taking control into my own hands.

During my school and varsity days I spent a lot of time and effort trying to fit in and be friends with the so-called 'cool' kids just so I could be popular. There was a flaw in this plan of mine. I tried to become popular by surrounding myself with people I did not even like as opposed to working on myself and becoming a nicer person. I took the control out of my hands and placed it in a group of guys who didn't have my best interest at heart.

When I reached the working world this 'searching for popularity' trend continued. I complained to my mom whenever she asked about my friends at work; "Ag, I don't really like them, but it's good for my reputation to be associated with them." My mom was confused by my rationale of picking these people and regarding them as 'friends' and constantly reminded me that "Birds of a feather flock together."

I saw that as a reassuring statement; if I am flying with popular people, then that must mean that I am popular myself? I was thoroughly mistaken. My mom explained to me; "When you surround yourself with people for long enough, you become like them. In your case you are constantly surrounding yourself with people who you don't like...soon enough you will become someone that you don't like!"

This shocked me. I had never looked at it like that before. I always assumed people would see me as one of the popular guys not as an arrogant prick – which was why I didn't like the 'cool' guys in the first place. That realisation coupled with the devastating Greg saga forced me to change the way in which I choose my friends. I wouldn't choose them on the basis of what they had or the fake perception they gave off, rather I would choose them for the real qualities they possess and whether I actually enjoyed their company.

Since changing my mind-set, I have built up a base of over twelve mentors in various areas of learning; strategic thinking, career building, managing conflict, self-awareness and speaking, just to name a few.

Most people thought I was crazy for having so many mentors, but my mom's words constantly reassured me; "Birds of a feather flock together." I knew that if I could surround myself with real people who I respected and who I thought were successful, I would become more like them.

I took the control from getting other people to build my credibility and personality and began to work on myself. I didn't need the 'cool' guys around me so that people would notice me or think I was popular. Instead I focused on myself and I became confident and assertive about what I believed in because I modelled people who I respected in those areas.

Mauro is one of my mentors. He is a person I look up to because of the way in which he respects women. He has made a huge impression on me. One day while grabbing a beer he said; "Every woman is a daughter in someone's eyes." It was a statement that has stuck with me ever since and something that I am reminded of whenever I am in the presence of a woman. He taught me what it meant to be a gentleman.

Surrounding yourself with the people you truly admire as opposed to a meaningless interaction with people you don't even like will help you model the characteristics you need to grow into the person you want to become.

At the end of the day you cannot decide or control how people will perceive you. You could take the easy route and surround yourself with the 'cool' guys and hope people won't see through your façade or lack of substance. Or you can take the road less travelled and claim back your reputation and hold it firmly within your own hands.

Work within your circle of influence to maximise the impact it will have on your own life otherwise you may risk being at the mercy of the puppet's strings. Work on the things that you can control. As Charles de Lint famously said; "You've got to find yourself first. Everything else will follow."

LIAM'S FIRING

On a lazy Wednesday afternoon work was standing still. A work colleague, John, and I decided to shoot the breeze for lunch in order to finish the unproductive day on a high. John had become a close friend in a short period of time since we were able to easily relate to each other.

We were both weird and different and that was the start of a very successfully friendship. I also enjoyed catching up with him because he constantly reminded me about the importance of choosing the right friends.

John was a person who never judged anyone based on what other people said about them. He would make a judgement of them based solely on his own experiences. I remember one Thursday afternoon John and I were relaxing in his office watching a funny YouTube video. A younger lady rushed into the office and screeched at John; "Did you hear, Liam is being fired."

I heard the news and a devilish smile crossed my face as I said softly to myself; "About freaking time." Please understand that I was not being a horrible person rejoicing in someone else's misery. In my view Liam really deserved what he got. He was the grumpiest, most unpleasant old man that had no time for anyone except himself. He once demeaned a shy developer's confidence at work by shouting at him; "You are too stupid to insult." This poor developer left weeks later out of embarrassment and his confidence was destroyed.

I was most surprised when I looked over at John to see his reaction to what I had thought was fantastic news. He frowned slightly and in an earnest voice said; "That's a pity, I hope Liam is ok." Both the news giver and I were stunned speechless. In our opinion Liam fully deserved what he had gotten, if not worse.

John didn't react with the anticipated glee everyone was expecting, even though he had been privy to many conversations where Liam's character had been questioned. As the younger lady left John called Liam and arranged a drink with him. I was taken aback by John's actions.

"What are you doing John? Don't you remember how rude he was to everyone?" – I said trying to shake him out of going for drinks. He calmly replied; "That's only one side of the story. Maybe he's a great guy and slightly misunderstood, I don't know? But I will find out for myself."

He has a remarkable ability not to judge a book by its cover, allowing each person a chance to redeem themselves. Only after spending time with a person would John decide if a friendship is on the cards or not. Luckily John agreed with us about Liam's foul personality after his drinks session. I laughed at John and said; "I told so." To which he replied; "Your right, he's terrible, but I had to see it for myself."

John inspired me greatly as he took charge in formulating his own opinions in his life. He could have easily accepted everyone else's opinion of Liam. Many people judged me when I first joined the company due to my vivacious and outrageous personality coupled with my hipster dress sense. Luckily he decided to get to know me before rejecting the version of who others assumed I was.

Surrounding myself with John helped me to value my own opinion about all aspects of life and the people in it. He taught me not to merely accept what others around me preached. He often said to me; "If being like everyone else makes you successful then why are there so few successful people in the world?" I soon learnt the power of not following the crowd and deciding things for myself.

THE COMMUNICATIONS DIRECTOR

After seeing the significant value that John had in my life I ensured that we spent many afternoons chatting and spending time together. He soon became and still is a very close friend who regularly joins me for a break away and who I can always confide in.

John told me that he saw a younger version of himself in me. When he was my age he also had ambitious goals but as he became more experienced his dreams started to shrink and become more 'realistic'. I felt privileged that John saw me like that and it connected us to a deep level of friendship. I wanted to share my ambitions with him because it reminded him of a stage in his life where the sky was the limit and dreaming was endless.

In the midst of talking about my current dream of writing a book, my excitement ran away with me and the volume of my voice exceeded normal decibels. My mind went on a rampage filled with exhilaration as I explained each chapter's purpose and how it would all tie in together.

John was impressed with my enthusiasm about the topic and said: "That's the kind of energy our leadership team needs in order to take this company to the next level." In a joking manner I blurted out; "Don't worry John, in two years' time I will be the Communications Director and show the leadership team some energy."

He giggled slightly and said; "Remember me when you get to the top." I chuckled in return, paused and asked in a somewhat serious tone; "Do you think it's possible?" John's smile turned into a mere grin; "It could be. I wanted to be the Human Resources Director at 30." "What happened to that dream?" – I asked. "I couldn't because there already was a Human Resources Director and she wasn't planning on leaving anytime soon. I would have to wait for her to leave in order to stand a chance."

It was a dilemma that I too may need to overcome if I want to become Communications Director. This was extremely demotivating for both John and myself as we had no control in fulfilling our dreams. We had to wait for someone else to make a career change and only then would it be possible. I sighed; "Ag why is our future determined by other people John?"

John glared at me and responded; "Don't ever say that again. You can still work on yourself so that when the time comes you can be the person who encompasses the right qualities and characteristics to be a Director of a company. Don't worry about what the current Director is doing, rather focus on you... make yourself an asset."

He smiled embarrassingly; "Don't wait like me for the opportunity to come, rather create the opportunity and get ready to pursue it as soon as it is available." I saw the fiery passion that John had for people, and specifically how he saw himself in me. I have no doubt that if John could speak to his twenty-four year old version of himself that he would have told him the exact same thing.

I was massively inspired and empowered by John. He helped me to stop worrying about what the current Communications Director was doing and to refocus on my goals instead. "Why focus your energy on waiting for the Communications Director to leave? That's time being wasted which could be spent on growing yourself into the right person for the job... be it at that company or another."

I immediately jotted down ideas and characteristics I would need to develop in order to become the right person for the job. After a meeting I went to the COO and told him about my ambitions of becoming a Director and asked his guidance in developing me to that level. I am now working furiously towards my goal and I am fuelled to the max. The power is back in my hands.

John helped me realise that as soon as someone is in your way of achieving your dreams you need to view your problem from a different perspective – one which enables you to make a difference. You cannot change circumstances outside of your control nor should the achievement of your goals be reliant on the actions of other people.

Until you focus your energy on your circle of influence you give the pen of your story to someone else, and you lose the authorship of your own story. As the saying goes; "I'm too busy working on my own grass to notice that yours is greener."

THE UNKNOWING ROLE MODEL

My younger sister Katherine and I were enjoying a pleasant drive home from Pretoria after spending some quality time with our parents. Our main topic of discussion was about the complexities of a work-life balance and time management.

I had just finished reading the book 'The 4-hour Work Week' by Timothy Ferris and I found it to be life changing. I have since incorporated some of the simple time management techniques and tools suggested in the book and have managed to reduce my office hours by half.

Katherine listened attentively to my story, hoping to gleam some of the knowledge. She was at a cross roads in her career. She has always been an ambitious person, however her current job and working hours were wholly unacceptable to her since she values spending time with her family and friends.

Katherine and her fiancé, Stef, were nearing their Wedding Day and Katherine was eagerly anticipating babies in the near future. "I can't imagine myself having a family if I continue working the long hours that my job expects of me" – She told me. I couldn't imagine what it would feel like to work on average ten – twelve hours a day.

I looked at Katherine in complete dismay, "Ten to twelve HOURS!?! Are you serious?" To which she embarrassingly nodded. I knew that Katherine was hard working but I never quite realised how hard working. That was insane.

I was so shocked by the devastatingly long work hours that I couldn't think of the tools and recommendations that I had learnt from the 4-hour work week. 'How do you keep up?' I thought to myself.

Katherine is often described as the happiest and bubbliest person anyone has ever met. I had to ask her; "How do you give everyone so much time and energy when you are so drained at work?" "I might not be able to control my working hours but I don't allow my work to control how I feel or treat the most important people in my life." – She replied gratefully.

In that moment I saw Katherine not as my sister but as an iconic role model, vital in my understanding of self-empowerment and control. She is such an inspiration to me because although she nearly works herself to death, there is never a task too difficult or a favour to unmanageable for her friends, family and fiancé.

Regardless of her time spent at work none of the people close to her get dropped by the waste line and always get the attention they are due. Above all, she regards the people in her life as her top priority.

I remember while growing up that Katherine had a tough time studying Accounting in her first year of varsity. She was literally behind a desk day in and day out for the entire year. I thought to myself that if I was in that situation I would have been the grumpiest person alive but as soon as Katherine exited the cauldron of despair her stressed mood instantly disappeared and she exuded a happy state of mind.

It was encouraging that she was able to put a genuine smile on her face, and in turn make those around her smile too, regardless of the difficulties she was experiencing... "You are my inspiration, you know that Kat?" – I said whilst pulling up towards her apartment. "Ah thanks Laurens, why do you say that?" – She blissfully asked.

I explained to her how I saw her, that she was just the icon of happiness regardless of the turmoil around her. "Thank you" – she said. "I think the key to my own happiness is the acceptance of things that I cannot control. I choose to be happy and I choose to control the feelings I have and the actions I take in all aspects of my life."

Katherine has always been the star of the family and has excelled in all elements of her life; be it sport, socialising or academics. I believe it's because of her positive mind-set. She focuses on herself and accepts everything else around her. She can't control the weather, how people act or what her work expectations are but she can put a smile on her face and be nice to people.

I strive to be like Katherine every day. She has a lively disposition and her positive attitude is contagious. She works within her circle of influence and accepts the rest. I am truly blessed to have a role model like her.

Through my dealings with different people from different walks of life and different circumstances I have learnt that you can effect change within your circle of influence. Everything else is completely out of your control and you can either accept that or fight a losing battle.

Trying to master everything and plan for all the scenarios will leave you demotivated, worried and will ultimately result in the fatal disease of failure.

We have so little time in our lives – to spend it focusing on the wrong things is pointless. Take control of your life because the truth is, it is in your control where and on what to focus. Your life is a product of your thoughts and actions.

[See exercises for this chapter at the end of the book]

9. IMPOSSIBLE TO PLEASE EVERYONE

We have all heard the expression it's impossible to please everyone, right? Bill Cosby took that expression one step further when he said "I don't know the key to success but the key to failure is trying to please everybody"

THE GINGER DISASTER

The best part of the Graduate Programme of the company was that you got to meet so many amazing people. Every day we were introduced to new faces and new departments. Obviously this also meant that we had to introduce ourselves to the new faces.

The first time I introduced myself I was like an Energiser bunny on a high; "Hi my name is Laurens, I studied at University of Pretoria and did a Computer Science Degree. It is so great to meet you. I can't wait to learn more from you." After about the fourteenth introduction this Energiser bunny slumped into a tape recorder-like sloth. "Hi, my name is Laurens, nice to be here. Looking forward to learn more."

We had just entered the sales rotation and the sales guys didn't like the introduction. "Laurens, that is really poor. The least you could do is tell us a joke." – One of the loud-mouthed salesman said. I don't know about you but whenever I have to tell a work appropriate joke I can only remember the dirty ones.

The ones that are only appropriate when you and your best mate are in a bar until four am and no one is even listening to you anymore. I went into a frenetic frenzy trying to think of an appropriate joke, but after twenty seconds of excruciating silence I cracked under the pressure and chose the least dirty one I knew.

> *A woman passes out while giving birth, as she wakes up she finds the doctor standing right in front of her with a concerned look on his face. The woman panics and screeches; "What happened!!!! Why do you look concerned, tell me what happened!" The doctor calmly unlocks his mouth and says; "Mam, I have some good news, but I also have some bad news. The bad news is your child is a ginger... the good news is it died."*

I was embraced with a Guinness Book of Records awkward silence. My cheeks chameleon'ed into a ripe red apple as the silence grew tenser. A lady, who I hadn't seen before the introduction, popped her head from behind the large sales men's bodies. She was in fact a ginger. After the meeting the lady had some choice words for me... words that I cannot legally put into this book.

I honestly can't blame her for her reaction because the joke was rude and quite inappropriate, but I also shouldn't blame myself. My intention wasn't to offend anyone, on the contrary I actually wanted to make people smile. Unfortunately not everyone is going to see things the way you see it but that doesn't mean that you are wrong.

Remembering that you cannot please everyone will lift a weight off your shoulders. You will just do what makes sense to you and let people react their own way based on their filters and backgrounds. Sometimes you have to do what you believe is good enough and accept that not everyone will agree.

I told my relationship manager mentor, Donve, about this story and asked her advice on how to resolve the situation and get the ginger lady to like me again. Donve had experienced a similar situation and learnt the hard way that a good intention doesn't always equal a good reaction when she unknowingly offended her domestic worker.

MONKEY

Donve has always called people she likes in her life 'monkey', for her it is a pet name of endearment. When she comes to work she calls all of her staff 'monkey', she even calls her manager 'monkey'.

She came home one day and caught her domestic in the kitchen cooking some lunch and she said; "Hello monkey, the food smells delicious, what are you making?" The domestic looked up as a disgust replaced her smile. "Did you just call me a monkey?" "Yes my little monkey" – Donve said blissfully unaware.

Her domestic stormed out of the room and left Donve puzzled. After a short discussion with her domestic Donve realised that 'monkey' was the furthest thing from a cute pet name to her domestic. Her domestic had seen the term 'monkey' as extremely offensive.

Donve didn't mean it in an offensive way though the domestic used her own filter on what Donve was saying. It doesn't mean that Donve was ugly or mean... she just has a different filter to her domestic. No one was right or wrong.

Donve said "It's important to realise that not everyone will see things the way you do but that doesn't mean that you are wrong. Understand that some people have filters based on their pasts and you can use that knowledge to better your communication with that person."

Donve still, to this day, calls me 'monkey', but whenever she sees her domestic she uses another term... 'Turkey'. Donve's domestic absolutely loves the term 'turkey' because her mother used that as a pet name for her.

It is important to know that people will not always see things your way based on their past experiences, backgrounds and belief systems. Reminding yourself that pleasing everyone is impossible will help you to remain true to who you are.

If you have the perspective that people are different, and that it's ok to be different, you won't take an insult personally. Rather take it as a lesson learnt about that person's filter and treat them accordingly. It is your intention that matters, not the way the person perceives it.

[See exercises for this chapter at the end of the book]

10. FACING THE FEAR WITH BELIEF

There is a very well-known tale that my dad shared with me when I was very young, and the story still rings true to me today. The story goes as follows; A Cherokee elder was teaching his grandchildren about life. He said to them, "A fight is going on inside me... it is a terrible fight between two wolves. One wolf represents fear, anger, envy, sorrow, regret, greed, arrogance, hatefulness, and lies. The other stands for joy, peace, love, hope, humbleness, kindness, friendship, generosity, faith, and truth. This same fight is going on inside of you, and inside every other person, too." The children thought about it for a minute. Then one child asked his grandfather, "Which wolf will win?" The Cherokee elder replied... "The one you feed."

It's scary to tackle the unknown, discover who we are and take control of our lives by motivating the right action and repairing the damaged roof. It will take a lot of patience and persistence just like conquering any other fear that you may face, be it rejection, chasing your dream or jumping off the bridge tied to a messily-knotted little bungee rope.

Fear will forever always be an opponent in your life, but you are the one who gets to decide how big the opponent will be. You can spend your whole life imagining ghosts, worrying about your pathway to the future, but all there will ever be is what's happening here, and the decisions you make in this moment, which are based in either belief or fear.

You dispel fear by not feeding it and feeding belief instead. Let's start by dispelling one of the most common fears that we possess, the fear that it cannot be done... that it is impossible.

IMPOSSIBLE IS AN OPINION

It was a cold winter's day afternoon as the dark, heavy ominous clouds peeked over the majestic Swiss Alps heading for the capital, Bern. Two young brothers, Steven and Paul, sat watching the storm brewing in anticipation of the first hints of snow fall. Both knew that as soon as the snow fell they would be transported to a winter's paradise.

Steven and Paul lived around the corner of a crystal lake which after the first snow fall turned into a seemingly steady frozen playground. They woke up the next morning with delight, the snow fall had been plentiful. They raced to where the frozen lake was and began to enjoy themselves like a shopaholic during a summer's sale.

Now as brothers usually do, they began to compete to see who could be the most dangerous without breaking their neck. Paul was only seven years old and was the first daredevil. He ran across the width of the lake in a flash and jumped head first into the snow embankment. Steven, the older brother, who was nine years old decided to step it up a notch and show Paul how a real man lives on the edge.

He ran in a circle around the lake and then did a handstand. Paul was speechless, and his excitement dropped into a dismay of disbelief as obviously Steven was winning. Steven came down elegantly from his handstand, his foot landed on a patch of thin ice and it shattered spreading a web of cracks around him. In an instant Steven had been sucked into the frozen water and the sub-zero temperatures paralysed his entire body.

The undercurrent of the lake dragged him underneath a thick solidified carpet of ice. Paul was the only person within a two kilometre radius that was able to help his stranded older brother. He jumped to his knees and began to punch the ice with an iron fist but alas this just left him with red a devastation on his hand and not an inch gained on the ice.

He frantically looked around for help and located a pine tree. He dashed over and broke off a branch. Paul then ran to his brother and began beating the branch on the ice with all of his might. Ten excruciating bashes later the ice splintered open and Paul dragged Steven out. Paul then collapsed out of exhaustion.

A few minutes after the paramedics arrived to stabilise both brothers. Once the boys were safe, the paramedics tried to understand how a seven year old boy was able to firstly break a branch off a tree and then use that branch to break through the ice. One of the paramedics couldn't believe it; "It's not possible. It would take a large man with an axe to do what he did... it is not possible."

An elderly gentlemen overheard this conversation, approached them and said gently; "I know how he was able to do that... because there was no one around him telling him that he couldn't do it."

People who can't do something themselves want to tell you that you can't do it either. They will want you to believe that it is impossible so that you won't even dare ask for it or try.

ASKING THE QUESTION

How often does life give you what you want on a silver platter? How often does your company give you the 100% raise that you want out of thin air? Probably not very often, right? Without asking for what you want you probably won't get what you are looking for. As Nora Roberts once challenged "If you don't go after what you want, you will never have it. If you don't ask, the answer will always be no. If you don't step forward, you will always be in the same place."

How often do we choose the path of fear disguised as practicality? What we really want seems so impossibly out of reach, that we never dare to even ask the universe for it. My dad, Walter, has mastered the art of complaining if he doesn't like something. For example, two weeks ago my dad invited the family to go for a celebratory dinner at an exquisite restaurant, he had just made a lucrative investment and wanted to share the good news.

We all gathered in the parking lot of the prestigious KOI restaurant in Sandton and began to rejoice in my dad's good fortune. A delightful smile possessed my dad as we walked towards the restaurant. As soon as we had entered the restaurant my dad's delighted smile turned into a disgusted sneer; "Ag no man, the music is too loud." Here we go again the family thought.

A waiter directed us to a table for six and within seconds of sitting down my dad raised his hand like the Queen of England expecting everyone to drop what they were doing to serve her dire need. The waiter, who knew my dad from previous dinners, reluctantly approached knowing my dad was going to complain. "Yes sir, how can I help you?" – The waiter kindly asked. "Ag you know man it's not a big deal but the music is just a volume or two too loud. Could you please turn it down slightly?" – My dad asked.

The waiter politely nodded and made his way to the music player. I turned to my dad in exasperation; "Dad, why do you always have to say something?" My dad looked slightly confused at first, and then he paused briefly while collecting his thoughts.

A polite gentle smile caressed his face as he replied; "Laurens, if I do not ask, the answer is anyway no." The proof was in the pudding as my dad almost always got his way, and in this case the music was turned down to a lower volume. To be honest I couldn't even hear the difference but my dad was pleased. This was all because he had asked, how simple.

The moral of the story is to at least provide the universe with the question, open yourself up to letting it provide it for you and if the universe doesn't get back to you right away, it's only because the universe is so busy fulfilling my order.

YOU CAN FAIL AT WHAT YOU DON'T WANT

When I was fourteen years old I was informed by my school that I needed to decide what my career was going to be, so that I could choose the appropriate high school subjects suited to that career. The school I attended was an extremely small private school with very limited options.

I approached my teacher in disappointment; "Mam I don't see subjects that are going to help me get my dream job." My teacher, Miss Moore, looked at me in confused amazement; "Oh now, are you sure? What is your dream job?" A giant smile crossed my face as I began to envisage my dream; "To be a professional dancer!" – I said glowing with excitement.

Miss Moore paused for a second as she sweetly smiled; "That's so sweet Laurens, though it is almost impossible to make a career out of dancing, you basically have to be the best or you won't be able to eat." I believed her as I knew no better and thanked her for her advice. I walked away with my shoulders drooping.

"Wait Laurens, isn't there something else that you would like to do?" – She enquired feeling heartbroken after squashing my dreams. "Well, I've always wanted to be famous like Will Smith and make a difference in the world." Miss Moore gazed at me with wonderment in her eyes as she listened to my confident dream.

"Sorry to do this again Laurens, but to become like Will Smith you have to have something extremely special about you. You're a clever boy, why don't you rather take the safe route and study engineering? Then after varsity you are guaranteed a job and steady income for the rest of your life."

Miss Moore, with genuinely kind intentions, convinced me to choose specific subjects in order to have engineering as an option. I told my parents of the conversation I had with Miss Moore and they had to agree with her; "You are special Laurens, *but* rather be realistic and achieve your goals than unrealistic and face disappointment."

Everyone asked me what it is that I wanted to be and proceeded to tell me what I couldn't be and I wasn't the only one. How many times have you been told your dream is silly, that it's impossible? "Rather take the safe route" was always the response as if the safe route is guaranteed. We are told that it is better to live a realistic, average and safe life then to take life on and be the difference we want in the world... but is average really the safe way?

Jim Carrey told a story of his past at a graduation speech he gave at MIM University. He said his dad, Percy Carrey, had aspirations of becoming an amazing comedian. All his friends and family saw his humorous potential and knew it was possible for him. I mean come on, if you have the same genes as Jim Carrey you are pretty much destined for comedy, anyone can see that.

Percy also knew in his heart that his passion lay in comedy but he felt that he couldn't make a living from comedy, that he couldn't support his family. Percy then decided not to follow his heart but rather to take the safe route instead and went on to study accounting. Percy graduated four years later with flying colours and went to work for a world renowned accounting firm as one of the rising stars.

When Jim Carrey was twelve years old the company went through a crisis and Percy was let go from his safe job. The family had to do whatever they could just to survive; borrow money from friends, accept food from the church... Jim Carrey ended this heart wrenching story by saying; "That day I learnt from my dad that you can fail at what you don't want... so you might as well go after what you love."

We are told that we must somehow become what we are not, sacrificing what we are to inherit the masquerade of what we will be. People will have great intentions when giving you advice, especially your family, but I don't want to live a safe life... do you? I want to reach the end of life having been worn out, scratched, battered and bruised screeching to a halt screaming; "WHAT A RIDE!!"

The only thing stopping us from being great is the fear of failure, but is that fear real? Is it that daunting that it cannot be faced? Or could it be a hyped-up fallacy?

FEAR IS FALSE EVIDENCE APPEARING REAL

I had a close friend at school, Marc, who would walk home on the same path every day. There was a menacing, vicious dog that would wait for him a kilometre from his house. The dog would chase him, barking aggressively and he would scare Marc into quiet desperation. He would confide in me about how terrified he was of the dog. He believed that the dog would likely one day kill him and he had no idea how to stop it.

One Tuesday morning he arrived at school with wet pants... the dog had done a number on his fear levels. He spoke to me at break with fierce determination in his voice; "I am sick and tired of this dog. Today I will fight back, I am going to grab a brick and throw it in front of the dog to scare him. Then he will leave me alone."

Marc began his travels on Tuesday afternoon with slight confidence as at least he had a plan. He arrived in the dreaded street and heard the dog's ominous bark. Marc saw the dog in the distance and his fear got the better of him as he sprinted for his house. On the way he ran past a construction site and saw many loose bricks. This reminded him of the deal he had struck with himself and he got a new motivation to fight his fear.

He grabbed one of the bricks, turned around and waited until the silhouette of the dog was in clear sight. The dog approached menacingly and Marc's hand was shaking. The dog was in clear sight now as Marc cocked his arm, just before throwing the brick he saw something that threw him off. The vicious dog that he dreaded was merely a Jack Russell and had no teeth. Marc dropped the brick and arrogantly walked past the dog saying; "Get out of my way, kid."

Often we choose the path of fear and build it up as a threatening monster that we couldn't dare face but are our fears really that overwhelming? Once Marc took ACTION he dispelled his fear, it was not nearly as daunting as he thought it would be. Perhaps the fear that you are facing is a small Jack Russell without any teeth? Maybe it's time to stop feeding the fear wolf and feed the belief wolf instead.

TAKE A CHANCE ON BELIEF

I remember the day I woke up and decided that I wanted to become an inspirational speaker. I immediately called up my best friend, Bradley, and shared with him the amazing news. Brad was so happy for me and invited me for a beer at his house, which I graciously accepted. As soon as I arrived at his house we embraced, opened up two chilled beers and psyched each other up with the endless possibilities.

Brad then asked me what my plan was... to which I had no answer. "I just thought it would be cool, I haven't gotten a plan yet." – I squeamishly said. Brad and I got to brainstorming and through the collaborative creative effort, a plan was devised. I would record a few short speeches to put onto YouTube in order to spread my messages. Bradley then took it upon himself to organise the entire shoot and did the editing of every single one of the forty short speeches that I had prepared.

Not long after the videos were shot Brad emailed them to me and I began uploading the videos. To be perfectly honest I was absolutely petrified of what people would say. I thought to myself what if they say; "Look at that idiot, who would ever listen to him?" I began to feed the fear by contemplating, 'Why would they listen to me? I haven't climbed Mount Everest, I haven't been through a traumatic experience and I haven't done anything significant. Why would anyone want to aspire to be like me?'

My fears were on a rampage eroding my confidence along way. In the midst of contemplating taking down the videos from YouTube my life coach, Bax, called me; "Hey Laurens, set up a meeting for us to catch up. I feel like we haven't spoken in a while." Perhaps it was fate, perhaps it wasn't but something told me to talk to Bax before taking down the videos and giving up on my dream.

I entered his office with the matured fears eating me up inside. I told him about the fears I have of others' opinions and what he said rang so true within me that I will never forget it. "How do you expect to have time to pursue your dream if you're spending so much time pursuing your fears instead? Why not take a chance on belief? With the belief that it is possible, you'll spring into action."

He continued to explain to me that once I take that first step of action I will begin to see hints of my inspirational dream become reality and a flame will be added to that ember of belief that I already possess... "It will become an unstoppable forest fire." – Bax ended.

It's a great thought-provoking question, why not take a chance on belief? How many times have you taken a chance on fear instead? Perhaps this will happen, perhaps I will fail, perhaps people will laugh at me... all the while putting yourself down... but what if none of that ever happens? What about taking a chance on belief? Perhaps I will succeed, perhaps I will positively impact people's lives and perhaps I am destined for greatness.

Isn't that way of thinking a lot more motivating to get you to at least try rather than worry about the potential failures? I remember the limiting fears that paralyzed me whilst out at a bar. I would see an attractive woman and just before I approach her my fears would come a knocking. Perhaps she has a boyfriend, perhaps she won't like my style, perhaps she will laugh at me... all the while saying the same thing WHY BOTHER TRYING?

Without trying there is absolutely no way of success and so it becomes a self-fulfilling prophecy. We automatically fail and the fear gets fed. Why not take a chance on belief? Perhaps she is single, perhaps she will like my look or perhaps nothing romantic will happen but maybe I make a cool new friend. Now I'm feeling motivated to at least try.

Fear is the proud bully in the playground but is a squeamish pup when the teacher action is present. Fear is False Evidence Appearing Real and once you take fear on face to face you will see the horrid Pit-Bull shrink down to a timid Jack Russell without teeth. As Mark Twain put it; "I've had a lot of worries in my life, most of which never happened." Ultimately most of the things we fear never come true anyway. Our fears are often misunderstood illogical statements that prevent us from doing what we know is right.

BRAZILIAN HEARTBREAK

In the year 2013 I had fallen hook, line and sinker in love. A beautiful, charismatic Brazilian beauty had stolen my heart and everything in my life made sense again. We could hardly bare to be apart for more than a day. When we were together it was like a drug of happiness we both so desperately desired. We believed that we would be the young lovers our older selves would someday reminisce about... though this was not necessarily the case.

Six months of pure bliss was followed by one month of unforeseen difficulty. It was our first rough patch, something all relationships experience at some stage, and she didn't feel that I was worth the effort of trying to make it work. A couple of fights later it all ended with a haunting phone call; "Sorry Laurens, I don't love you anymore..." I was broken.

I went from feeling on top of the world to being a miserable worthless morsel. A spiritless soul had possessed my state of mind as I zombie'd around for weeks on end. Everyone I came into contact with could immediately tell something was wrong.

They would always politely ask what was getting me down and after I told them the heartbroken tale everyone's reaction was the same; "Don't worry Laurens, there's plenty of fish in the sea. Just let her go man, just move on." But just letting her go didn't seem such a simple thing to do for me.

I began to notice how people could so easily give advice to other people; "Follow your dreams!" "Ask for the raise." "Move on, you deserve better." Without being able to take that advice when they were going through the tough time themselves.

I asked my emotional intelligence coach, Jess, why this was the case? Jess said; "It's because the person giving the advice is not emotionally invested in the situation. To them it doesn't really matter what the consequence of the action is and therefore they don't fear doing what is right." Again Jess hit me with a keen insight.

I knew that letting my ex go would remove the feelings of discomfort from me and make me feel better. However, I associated fears with letting her go and it clouded my vision. Jess and I reminisced some stories of my ex and my relationship until a climatic point where he asked a targeted question; "What fear do you have of letting her go?" I paused for an extensive period as I needed time to understand and name the fear, something that I had never done before.

"I guess I'm scared I'll be successful in letting her go." – I muttered. "Interesting... and why does that scare you?" – Jess enquired further. "What if I let her go, move on and in so lose any chance of having her in my life forever?" – I asked. "Okay, so you fear moving on from her because you might actually move on?" – Jess confirmed. "Yes. I know it sounds silly." – I answered feeling embarrassed. "How would it make you feel if you did move on?" – Jess asked. "Simply great." – I enthusiastically replied.

Jess had a devilish smirk across his face, and I was blushing as I reflected on the conversation. "That's such a stupid fear isn't it?" – I said. Jess just laughed and nodded empathically. Sometimes our fears are these absolutely pathetic illogically statements we use to prevent us from taking the correct action.

I'm not saying it's easy to let someone that you love go but at least acknowledging the fear and putting it into proper perspective is the right step. Our fears are not always as realistic as we first think and therefore do not deserve the priority we give them in our lives. Don't let the illogical statements prevent you from action because action is the best antidote to tackling fear.

<u>CURING FEAR WITH ACTION</u>

How many attempts do parents give their baby to walk before telling them to just give up? How many parents, after a couple of weeks say;

> "Ah come on Jimmy, it's not that hard."
> "You're doing it wrong!"
> "Time to give up, it's not possible."
> "Stop it now Jimmy, you're getting in people's way dammit!"

I would guess none, otherwise that parent should be given the worst parent of the century award.

The baby tries and tries and tries until he reaches his goal... never giving up. The beauty is that virtually every baby turns into a walking adult because they don't stop trying when they are tired, down and out... they stop when they are done, when they have learnt to walk. Imagine you took that stance in life. "I won't stop until I finish." Do think anything would be able to stop you?

Take a chance on believing that you can achieve your goal even though this might not change the possibility for failure. At least it will get you to spring into action which would reveal the silhouette of the daunting fear to actually being a Jack Russell without teeth. Your confidence will grow and you will discover how to do it better and better and better until you are the best.

Colonel Sanders, as mentioned in previous chapters, was sixty five years old and living from pension pay check to pension pay check but he wanted more. He knew he deserved more. He took the famous family chicken recipe and went from one chicken fast food outlet to the next trying to sell the recipe.

He said to the managers of the stores; "I don't want any money for the recipe, I only want 1% of the sales of my recipe." Every manager slammed the doors in his face, but he never gave up. He continued with persistence and enthusiasm from one store to the next with the same result, BANG. He was rejected over 1000 times and still did not give up.

On his 1009th attempt a store bought into the recipe and look where KFC is today. "It is impossible to fail if you never give up!" As long as you are trying you will get better, you might not strike it rich at first but with every step you take you get closer to the end of the rainbow. Never give up, just try again and tweak your strategy as needed.

Never give in to fear, keep fighting until it comes down to size but never let fear win. As you feed it, it will grow and become a violent raging Pit-Bull defining your life. This is your life, you must take charge of the fear!

NEVER LET FEAR WIN

Jean, my close work colleague, and I often shot the breeze with a coffee to start the day off. Eight am 6th October and as if rehearsed Jean enters the cubicle and says; "A small coffee'ke?" To which I replied with a wide grin coupled with an enthusiastic shriek; "Hell yeah!" and off we went. We each grabbed our preferred poison, for Jean it was black coffee, two sugars and me Rooibos Tea, three sugars.

The balcony was our lookout point, it had a fantastic view as far as the eye could see. We felt like commanders. He asked me about my weekend, to which I had a hesitant reply. That previous weekend I had cowardly surrendered to my fears. I wanted to write 1500 words of my book but got caught up in my fear, which led to my down fall. I kept saying to myself; "What if what I write isn't good enough?" This then eventually led me down the path of doubt and procrastination. He grinned as he was well aware that I was letting fear win.

He told me the story of his three year old daughter, Elana, who went swimming in a friend's pool the past weekend. "Elana was completely petrified of the water, and she would only let me put her feet into the water. After about three minutes she began to splash, play and muck around like any curious three year old. Ten minutes later and Elana's confidence took her to laps around the pool. She cramped slightly in her left calf and panicked – fearing that she would drown in the deep end." – Jean said dramatically.

Jean quickly grabbed Elana out of the water and placed her safely on dry land. Elana ran straight to her dad's legs and hugged them skin-tight; "Never again papa!" Jean heard these words and wondered if this fear would grow into a bigger than necessary fear later on in life. Perhaps she will remember this day as far worse than it was and create a mental block to swimming in a pool again.

He grabbed Elana against her will and went with her into the deep end of the pool. She screeched and demanded to be put on dry land again but Jean refused and continued to reassure her. After a couple of minutes Elana was laughing like nothing had even happened and swam on her own again. Jean said; "Rather than let fear win, conquer it by striking early."

A friend of my sister's, Sandy, was very keen on horse riding. Sandy wanted desperately to be a world champion and practised hard for it. Every morning she was the first on the field and the last to leave the field. She never feared any of the horses. One of the horses that they owned was approximately sixteen hands, which in English is around two and a half metres. Samson, the horse's name, was an infamous massive black horse that took no prisoners.

Sandy being a mere one and a half metres tall jumped on Samson as though he were a little pony. Her confidence portrayed through Samson as he blindly followed her every direction. After watching in amazement at Sandy's control I asked her; "Aren't you scared to fall off? That horse is huge!!"

Sandy giggled as she looked over at Samson; "He's harmless. When I was seven years old I was in my first competition. My horse at the time, Mystic, went against my orders and flung me to the ground. I hit the ground painfully hard and feared climbing back on. I looked around and saw all the judges looking at me and just got on the horse fearing any more gazes of disapproval. I finished the rest of my show and afterwards felt amazing. I was never again scared of falling off a horse." She fought the fear early on, without growing it into an obstacle of epic proportions.

We have to fight failure every day to bring it back down to size. If we avoid it and let it grow it turns a molehill into a mountain, a Jack Russell into a Pit-Bull. The only cure for fear is ACTION, consistent ACTION.

TAKE FEAR ON DAY BY DAY

Once you have grabbed that brick, turned around and faced your fear you would have grasped that your fear is not the ominous monster built up in your mind. The challenge now is not letting fear grow into that ominous beast. Most of us are in the habit of imaging the worst case scenario. We naturally take chances on fear, as it's what we know best, and we begin to feed the hungry beast as it diligently grows.

Adrian, my varsity counterpart, and I spent many long nights out at clubs in the hope of meeting a jaw-dropping, beautiful girl. We entered the club chests pushed out, dressed like the modern day John Travolta and in pursuit of sufficient liquid confidence to sooth the flirting process. We always began with a minor Jack Russell fear; "That girl might have a boyfriend."... But as the night progressed, we hesitated acting and activated the feeding of the little Jack Russell.

Soon the Pit-Bull had paralyzed us with anxiety;

"She has a boyfriend."
"She's too pretty."
"She won't like me."

All and all saying the same thing in a different way; "I am not good enough." The lack of action gave us more time to give fear a chance, gave us more time to imagine scenarios of failure and in so destroy our confidence.

A few weeks of anxiety filled nights passed before I picked up the brick. We again walked into our favourite night club, TY's. We began with our usual approach to the night; our chests were out and proud, dressed to the nine's and in the pursuit of some liquid confidence.

I saw a girl that seemed interesting and approached her immediately. We chatted for a couple of minutes but it became clear to both of us we were only destiny for friendship. We went our separate ways and Adrian and I grabbed a well-deserved drink.

The rest of the night I didn't imagine trials and tribulations, I fed off the confidence that the girls around me weren't huge Pit-Bulls ready to destroy me. I grabbed a brick and turned it onto my fear while realising the fear was unworthy of the status that I gave it. It was a liberating experience and one that I remember fondly.

Many nights followed after that illuminating night where fear got the better of me and that will happen to you as well. Sometimes we give in to the fear and it paralyses us... that's ok. Rome was not built in a day, but it was built one brick at a time. When you are faced with fear try grab that brick to stop the beast. Each time you do it your confidence will grow.

We have to fight the fear at every step otherwise it will run our lives, ruin the chance to fulfil our dreams? The only real solution is to continually grab that brick, make it a habit. As your confidence of facing your fear improves you will start to master taming the beast to a manageable Jack Russell without teeth.

By not acting out of fear we begin to erode our self-esteem. Eleanor Roosevelt had her own method of handling fears and to motivate the right action; "I believe that anyone can conquer fear by first doing three things: Do it once to prove to yourself that you can do it. Do it a second time to see whether or not you like it. And then do it again to see whether or not you want to keep on doing it." She said that by the time you have accomplished the third step, you have conquered the fear.

Once you have taken it to that level where you know you want to keep on doing it, then you need to fight that fear every day... starting with Monday, don't let fear take the steering wheel. You see Monday is going to walk in with that smug look on its face as if to say "Welcome back little boy, let's make it another good Blue Monday."

Imagine yourself grabbing that metaphorical brick shouting back at Monday; "HELL NO!! That's not how it's going to happen today Monday. It's my turn, my right and my responsibility to run this day. I'm going to be the best I can, pursue my dream, believe in myself and give you payback for so many prior blue Mondays!" Monday will be shocked, even speechless.

After you have run that day and taken the steering wheel away from fear, Monday will be like a pierced balloon, deflated. Tuesday will be next. You can politely sit Tuesday down, smile graciously and explain how Monday just left with its tail between its legs and that unfortunately you are next.

You welcome Wednesday by the door; "Please Wednesday come in. Sit down. Would you like a glass of water?" "I'm not particularly thirsty" – Wednesday will reply. "Well it's going to help swallow *your doomed* pill" – You'll insist.

Thursday will have already heard the news about the past three days and will be terrified, crying the night before and dreading imminent doom. This will probably be the easiest of days. Your confidence will be soaring and the fear fading… boom, write Thursday off as a success. By Friday it's already the weekend and things are happening. Five pm comes around and you warn the weekend "I'm ready, bring it on."

It all starts with conquering fear that first time, and mastering individual moments. You then gain momentum and defeat fear by taking action day by day. Those days will turn to weeks, weeks to months and months to years and it will be impossible for you to be stopped from reaching that dream that you always believed was unreachable. Its starts with the only moment that you can control, the here and now. Don't let fear win!

Napoleon Hill once said: "Whatever the mind can conceive, and believe, the mind can achieve". The disbelief of others will be leftover debris when we finally decide to smash through the limits of what we thought we were capable of. If you can't see the potential in yourself to achieve your dreams, get a better mirror, look a little closer and stare just that little bit longer.

There is greatness inside of you. While in pursuit of your dreams you will build a cast to protect your heart from the disbelievers and you will sign that cast yourself; "They were wrong." THEY HAVE TO BE WRONG. In the end we will graduate from the class of "WE MADE IT", and the echoes of "impossible" will die away like a whisper in a whirlwind. Belief will always be a stronger force than fear.

Fear is an ugly beast that is, more often than not, built up to be more daunting than it actually is. Change your perspective from focusing and feeding the fear to focusing and feeding your belief. You most likely will spring into action and conquer the Pit-Bull, one brick at a time.

I have used the perspectives defined in this chapter to great effect. It has propelled me to create the reality that I have always wanted. I have been blessed to start living the life I have always dreamed of in a matter of two years. I went from being a graduate to speaking on a global stage enjoying the perks of financial freedom.

I saw the life I wanted, not the life I had. Through countless hours of mentoring and reading books, I used perspectives that gave me confidence and motivation to achieve, not those that stunted growth and vision.

Clive was an inspiration in my life in helping me see life not as it should be but as it could be. He went from a teary victim in his story to the hero who saved the day smiling. The power is within your hands, it's the decisions and actions that you take that write the story of your life. If you do not act, that is still your choice. If you allow others to stand in the way, it is your choice to not work in your circle of influence.

Clive had a choice, as we all do, with the perspective he choose in taking flight. We all have the power to see things in a different perspective, we have proven that with the cell phone example, now it's up to you to choose the ones that are most beneficial to you.

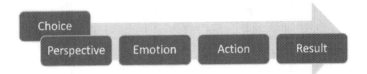

You must start with the end in mind, what result do you want to achieve? What action is going to get you that result, what emotion drives that action? Then CHOOSE the perspective that enables your feelings to be channelled in the right way! Whether you're upset or motivated, either way it is your choice, so why not choose the one that is more beneficial?

Reality is not fixed, fact or forever. We can alter the way we see the world to get motivated and achieve the unlimited greatness within all of us.

The point of this entire section is to change the way you interpret your reality. At the end of the day a phone will always remain a phone, the only thing we can do to change the phone into an alarm clock is to perceive it in a different way.

The above perspectives are tools that I have used and now teach to others to examine alternative views on reality. This doesn't mean that the reality is not tough, but you have got to ask yourself if viewing your reality as tough is helping you achieve your goals, helping you achieve your greatness.

The ultimate lesson that one needs to learn in order to make use of changes in perspective is that it doesn't change reality, it changes how you interpret and therefore how you feel. As you know feelings translate into actions. If you are determine to act you will need to feel that it's possible and that you are near to your goal, otherwise your determination will wane.

I am not saying that you MUST use all of the perspectives but promise me one thing; try them out at least once and if they don't work then discard them and leave it be, but if they work then I say USE IT. Helping yourself feel good in every situation has a great benefit to your body, mind and soul.

It is up to you to either let a little friendly tripping over the broom ruin the day or inspire an uplifting change to soar to new heights. The power ultimately lays in your hands.

[See exercises for this chapter at the end of the book]

CHANGE DOESN'T LAST UNLESS WE LAST

It's great that you have gotten this far in the book and I commend you. I hope that you have found value in the perspective tools described above and that you have completed the tasks at the end of the book in order to internalise them. These tools are not like riding a bike, it is something that without practise can be forgotten... it takes continuous practise and hard work to remain happy. No one said that it would be easy, but they did promise that it would be worth it.

In order for the change to be permanent our actions must be permanent. If we want to change our mind-sets to observing abundance and gratitude in our lives then we must open ourselves to various perspectives that promote appreciation every day. If you, for example, take the task of gratitude of 3, in the Exercises chapter, and do it for a couple of weeks you will see the results in your increased happiness, but if you stop the gratitude of 3 your mind will revert back to the more regular habit of taking things for granted... and happiness will remain the moving target.

Every time you take action you build a pathway in your brain. Once you practise the action of gratitude of 3 you build that appreciative pathway, though if you stop your brain will automatically go to the strongest pathway which is taking things for granted, a habit that has been ingrained over years. The mind works like the path of least resistance, the biggest pathway will always be unconsciously followed. We must make a conscious effort to break the old pathway and create a stronger pathway of the desired behaviour.

Let's begin making your change permanent by building the strongest path of the desired behaviour.

CHAPTER 4

MAKING YOUR CHANGE LAST

A habit is something that you do on a default basis. It is your habits that determine your life, as Stephen Covey said in his book, 7 Habits of Highly Effective People, "We become what we repeatedly do."

A habit can be that you bite your nails when you are driving, obsessively wash your hands after each meal or perhaps that you speak with your mouth full when you are excited about a topic. Habits aren't only negative like the ones mentioned, they can also be healthy, helpful and positive like always saying thank you, making your bed in the mornings or putting your dish in the dishwasher after use.

I always wake up more or less the same time for work and my behaviour from when the alarm clock sounds to when I leave for work is almost identical every single time. I sleepily drag myself out of bed and press the snooze button on the alarm clock... at least three times. On the fourth ring my mind clicks, and the routine of getting out of bed kicks in.

I groggily walk to the bathroom and begin my ablutions, which consists of a five minute shower coupled with brushing of teeth, hair and finally a quick full body spray. This is a process that I need no motivation for and is often done in a completely unconscious state... it requires no effort.

Wouldn't it be cool if you were in the habit of being great every day and it was so indoctrinated into your life that it required no effort, just like the washing process? It would take almost no effort to be amazing, successful and an expert in your industry because doing it would be second nature. We all wash ourselves every day without a second thought, right? It means it's possible to have habits running our lives, why not correct course and use the powerful influence of habits to achieving your goals?

We can change our psychology/perspective using the power of habit. Think back quickly to the last time a taxi unrightfully pulled in front of you, you had to screech to a halt preventing a crash which would ultimately cause a hassle in your life, what would your instant thought be? Probably that of irritation and wondering where he had bought his licence. It would take no effort to feel irritated, it would just come naturally. The way you see the world is all based on how you have always seen the world and changing that is like changing a habit.

It would be crazy for me to think that you have to wash yourself once and then you would be clean forever, right? The same thing applies to your happiness, you can't just have one good thought every now and again and expect to enjoy a happy life.

We have to work at being happy, positive and getting into the right frame of mind every day of our lives. Eventually, like the routine washing process, becoming happy will become second nature and will require no extra effort.

The great thing is that you can quickly tell when you need to change your thinking. If you don't shower for a little while it becomes obvious to you and everyone around you that you smell. You will see it on their faces and smell it. If you're in a bad mood people will most likely react negatively towards you and you would feel bad yourself. Changing your perspective to create the game in a winnable way is needed every day, it should be as consistent as you're washing routine.

Our habits are the things we are accustomed to doing every day. They are the things we are most comfortable doing and are a powerful force in shaping our lives. You are currently a product of your habits, if you want something better for your life then it's time to change your habits... let's find out how.

THE STALLION AND THE PORKER

Imagine walking into regular mall close to your house. Your mom has asked you to grab a bit of food from Woolworths just before the guests arrive for yet another enjoyable family dinner party. On way out of Woolworths a haunting aroma teases your nostrils. Your body automatically follows as your nose leads the way.

100 metres away, and approaching, you see the world famous red KFC logo and you thank your nose for its superb powers; "Dinner will only be in forty five minutes, I'll be hungry by then" – You rationalise while ordering a small portion of delicious zinger wings. While waiting for your zestful zinger wings you begin to watch the people entering

and leaving the KFC making 'guestimate' judgements about their lives.

If you were to see a very large overweight man delightedly rush into the KFC what would your initial thought be? 'He comes here often' – or some form of that opinion. Next you see a slim, fit and well-groomed young stallion approaching the counter. What would your initial judgement of him be? Perhaps 'he's buying food for a friend.' 'He's just been to gym and deserves a treat.' Again something similar to rationalise how a slim guy can remain slim after eating KFC.

The chances are your initial judgements, though I don't approve of judgements, would be accurate as our lives are a product of our habits. The larger overweight porker probably spends less time in the gym than the fit stallion. There is a high probability that the larger man eats take-away more regularly than his fit counterpart.

The large man is not fat because he eats KFC once a year and the rest of the year he counts calories and the stallion is not fit because he sits in front of the TV the whole day enjoying a never-ending feast of potato chips. What we do on a regular basis, our habits, manifest into our reality.

Our habits manifest into reality, it is what we do every day that makes the difference. A habit is formed by continuous repetitive action so that the mind grows familiar with that action and turns it into a routine task, like washing – which the mind is so familiar with that it takes almost no motivation to make it happen. It is a well-known fact that it takes twenty one days to create a habit... it takes twenty one days to CHANGE YOUR LIFE.

It is also true that a person must adopt certain traits in order to excel in certain jobs. A salesperson must be able to deal with rejection and be highly motivated by money. An accountant must enjoy working with numbers, excel spreadsheets and keeping track of every little detail. A manager must embody leadership skills and motivation abilities...

Some of these habits can be intrinsic – something that has always come naturally to you. I'm sure you've seen that one person who was just born to be a salesperson. The classic 'he could sell ice to an Eskimo' kind of person. He has the habit of understanding people and influencing them embedded in his nature. It is something that he has always done and it's been indoctrinated into him through his parents, schools and past experiences.

Some people just naturally fit into certain roles but that is not to say that you have to have these qualities in order to become a salesperson, accountant or manager. The necessary traits to be successful can be developed through repetitive tasks, they can be learnt and replaced. By changing what you do every day you can change who you are and how you act, by changing your habits you can change your life.

You can become a great sales person without having the people skills when you first start. You may have a fear of rejection but as you learn to handle rejections and come out realising that it's not the end of the world your confidence will grow. If you do not quite understand the product or how to influence someone you can constantly ask for help and model other successful salespeople until you learn the trade and selling will become natural to you.

Habits can be learnt and unlearnt, replaced and refined. Our brains grow depending on what we do most often. For example taxi drivers in London develop an unusually large spatial memory as they have to navigate the complex landscape of London's street every day. London is not based on a grid structure and therefore an ordinary person's spatial memory would not suffice, but because taxi drivers do it every day their minds have developed like that.

Your mind has created strong pathways to form your current habits. Washing yourself is easy and needs no motivation because your mind has built up that part of the brain. If you want to make a desired action a habit, you needs to practise it every day... to the point where it needs no motivation to get it done anymore. Changing a habit can be as easy as changing your environment.

THE LAWYER CURSE

I have a close friend, Adam, who is a perfect example of someone whose habits had changed through what he did every day. Adam was the saint of compassion at our school and everyone saw him becoming a profound psychologist whose comforting nature would convince anyone to accept advice. He was the type of person that saw the best in people and enjoyed making positive assumptions in every situation.

At school he was obviously very popular with his kind nature and easy-going demeanour, though this kindness did at times backfire on him. One time we all went to a random person's house party and a gay guy tried to make a move on him. Adam was taken aback by this guy's reasonably forceful effort but he didn't react with aggression or a punch... rather he calmly told the guy; "Sorry man, I'm not gay."

Adam had such a positive nature that I thought it was a waste when he decided to study law. When I confronted him his argument was that he could effect change in people's lives through being a lawyer; "I could become a Human Rights lawyer and protect vulnerable people by fighting for their rights in a court of law." – He argued.

Now, every parent would argue with me, there is actually a large downside to studying law. The prospects of the TV series, Suits, which we have taken as truth for the legal world, poorly defines the actual reality of the common law student.

After Adam's first six weeks of starting law we went for a drink to let off a bit of steam. He explained that the first day of class you are introduced to the concept of critical thinking. You are given a case study of a person who is without a doubt innocent but told that you must find an argument to fight against his obvious innocence.

The case given to Adam was that of an elderly lady who was walking over a pedestrian crossing when a frenzied drunk driver speedily ran her down, and he had to defend the clearly guilty driver. Adam looked at this case in puzzlement as there was just no way that the pedestrian was in the wrong.

His teacher explained that in court your opposition will create scenarios that lean so overwhelming towards one side that you must create another overwhelming version to convince the jury to see the full picture.

Adam with the help and direction of his teacher was able to find fault in the seemingly innocent gentle lady. The following weeks of constant critical analysis added a negative filter to his thinking based on the experience of that first class. When Adam joined me for a drink his kind, positive and gentle nature had been poisoned by a negative fog.

The waitress was taking slightly long to collect our drinks order and he immediately began interpreting her lateness and preached to me as if I was the jury about to sentence her; "She has taken well over the expected time and is currently enticing the customer, me, to leave without ordering. If the service isn't up to scratch then many customers might leave and the coffee shop will lose money and potentially close down. That means that many innocent people will lose their jobs because of this girl's tardiness."

I looked at him in complete shock as he had never before said a negative thing about anyone. He had been constantly surrounded by other negatively focused lawyers, indoctrinated in class with critical thinking and analysis and it had begun to affect his perspective. As Adam's studies progressed his happy-go-lucky nature and care-free positive attitude morphed into an adversarial attitude.

He couldn't separate his personal life from his studies and by the end of his second year he found himself unconsciously seeking an alibi from his girlfriend about the night she stayed out later than they had agreed. As soon as the alibi was given Adam created a compelling story contradicting her arguments. It was as if Adam saw every situation as though it were a courtroom filled with suspicious jury members.

I had seen him only six weeks after starting law and already his habits were changing. He was spending every day with like-minded critical thinkers all being taught how to look at every situation through a lens of pessimism. After the two year mark Adam's nature had developed the traits needed to be a fantastic lawyer.

After his studies Adam and I grabbed another drink to catch up and the kind-hearted, positively natured Adam was back. He had spent a lot of time reflecting on his life after his girlfriend left him and he realised that he had been engulfed by the lawyer way of living.

He told me; "I couldn't control myself after a while. Everything around me was a composition of stories that needed to be more compelling than the last. It was what I did every day and it became second nature... I didn't even know that I was doing it after a while."

Adam's habits changed because of what he was doing every day. If you sing every day of your life your vocal chords will become stronger, your hearing will become more attuned to the right pitch and your singing will undoubtedly improve. It is not what we do every now and again but what we do every day that makes the difference in our lives.

Habits can take us down completely different paths. Adam went from a kind-hearted, gentle person to a more critical being with an ability to argue multiple versions of the same story within a few weeks of changing his environment. Luckily he saw his short-comings and brought back the personality we all adored. Adam is now a fantastic lawyer and leaves the critical analysis in the courtroom, where he is enormously successful.

If you are serious about changing your life you must understand that it will not happen in one day. You can't go to the gym and after one session be instantly fit. However, if you commit to a gym program, get a motivational instructor and continuously build the habit of exercising regularly you will become fitter in less time than you expected.

It takes twenty-one days to learn a habit, according to Shawn Achor. To change your in life twenty-one days doesn't sound like a long time, does it? It's an investment of twenty-one days of your life where you have to force yourself and after that it will come as naturally as showering before work, cycling twice a week or praying before bed. Twenty-one days of the 30 000 odd days that most humans live really amounts to almost nothing. It is less than 0.001% of your life span.

That is a short time to make a difference, a lasting difference, wouldn't you agree? The difference between smelling bad in the morning and feeling fresh every day. The difference between dozing in front of the TV and energetically leaving the spinning class. The difference between feelings of spiritual unease or fulfilment before bed.

Start with a clear idea in your mind about where you want to be in three weeks' time (twenty one days) and then determine what you need to do every day to make that happen. Don't get too absorbed with the three week plan, focus on doing what you need to do today to build the right habit.

RPM – RESULTS, PURPOSE AND MAP

Tony Robbins is the world's most renowned inspirational speaker and peak performance coach. He also happens to be my role model and coach through audio books.

In his book 'Get The Edge' he explains a formulated approach to self-motivation which he calls the RPM; Results, Purpose and Massive Action Plan. He relates this process to a car's RPM meter. The car's speed is in direct proportion to its RPM, therefore the higher the RPM the higher the performance will be. The greater our RPM the greater our motivation will be to achieve our goals.

Tony Robbins is an absolute genius in the field and has coached and trained over four million people around the world. He often says in his tapes; "I would be a complete idiot if after thirty-five years of experience I don't see patterns in human behaviour." He has formed this program based on thousands of experiences and focus groups and if you put to practise his methodology you will see MASSIVE results.

RESULT

The first part of the RPM process is to shift our focus from the activity to the result. For example, imagine that you wanted to lose weight. The activity you might choose to achieve losing weight is to go cycling for twenty minutes every day. The result is losing the weight.

If your focus is on the activity of cycling every day it could be potentially destructive. If your bike broke down or you got a slight injury in your thigh which restricts cycling, then you couldn't achieve your goal. Whereas focusing on the result, losing weight, keeps your options open to various avenues of exercise, barring a bit of bad luck with your bicycle. The result is the WHY that motivates us during the pain of the HOW.

Another reason to look at the result is that it can motivate you in the tough times. The activity of cycling is not always the nicest prospect when it's cold and wet outside though the prospect of surprising your significant other with a six pack ripped body in the December holidays might spark the drive needed to jump out of bed and get into action.

Focus on the result and not the activity. The mind-shift change will allow you flexibility in achieving your goals. If you are faced with a challenge in one activity you can change your strategy and try another activity, you won't be restricted by one path to success.

Purpose

When you know WHY you are doing something, it takes away the difficulties of the HOW.

My speaking coach, Richard, is forty-five years old with a new-born baby. Talk about a difficult age to raise a new baby. He told me that the first six weeks of a baby's life is like going through hell and high water. All the baby does is poop, eat, sleep, cry, repeat... for six long weeks. During the six week process you almost get no interaction from the baby except for crying, "I felt like a zombie for six weeks... it's the closest to hell I ever wanted to get to." – Richard explained.

His long face turned into a picture of pleasure as he said "After those six weeks something quite amazing happens. She looks up at you with her soulful curious eyes and begins to smile for the first time." Richard paused as he reflected back to that moment, his cheeks reddened... "That's when I knew why I was going through all of the pain for her." The moral of the story is when we know why we are doing something it takes away the pain of doing it.

It is the WHY, not the HOW, that is the motivating force to produce the results needed to achieve our goals. In the 1900's Samuel Pierpont Langley set out to create the first flying machine and was destined for inevitable success... or was he? Samuel had all the ingredients needed to be successful; he was a mathematics professor from Harvard, he had powerful friends in government and unlimited resources (money, knowledge, and people).

Only a few hundred kilometres away Wilbur and Orville Wright were hard at work in building their very first flying contraption. The only resources that they had were enthusiasm and a strong why, nothing else; no government grants, no high-status connections, not even a college education.

In the end it was the Wright Brothers who amazed a small group of people on the 17th of December 1903 by piloting the first take-off the world has ever seen. It wasn't luck. They were able to truly inspire and motivate their team to go beyond their limits because they started with the why.

Think about a tough situation in your life. What is the WHY that is keeping you going or could keep you going? I've had some dark moments in my inspirational speaking journey. The worst was when I told my dad about my dreams and he thought I had lost touch with reality, he was furious. There was a brief moment where I felt as though he had disowned me. The only thing that kept me going was my WHY.

1. To walk in the footsteps of entrepreneurship like my role model, my dad.
2. To prove to my sometimes pessimistic family that anything is possible if you believe in yourself.
3. Lastly I believe each one of us has the ability and the responsibility to leave the world a better place than we once found it and speaking is my way of bettering the world.

That WHY got me through the toughest times of my journey thus far. I believe that without knowing the WHY and using it to my advantage I would not have had the courage to continue. When you are going through hell it's the WHY that keeps you going. Find out the WHY of what you are doing and use it in your moments of obscurity. Have your reason come first and the answers will follow.

MAP

The MASSIVE ACTION PLAN is a concept that Tony Robbins presents in many of his life-changing seminars. Tony explains that absolute clarity is needed when chasing goals. As we all already know in the pursuit of our goals we will be challenged by obstacles that will temporarily halt our progress. Tony says that during the tough times we need our focus to be on the result, have a clear purpose and have a clear path forward towards success – an action plan. "Reasons come first, answers come second."

"Failing to plan is planning to fail" – Alan Lakein. It is common knowledge that the clearer your goal and path to success the more guaranteed you are to achieve that goal. If I were to say that I wanted to earn more money next year what is the guarantee that I would achieve that goal? Almost none. I haven't specified how much money, by when I must earn that extra income and what the other constraints may be. I wouldn't know if I had achieved the goal. Let's get practical with our dreams.

<u>GOAL SETTING</u>

DREAM UNREALISTICALLY AND UNREASONABLY

Before one starts with goal setting one must first practise the art of unrealistic and unreasonable dreaming.

Goals are the achievements we want in our life and because we are all destined for greatness shouldn't our goals be great as well? Think about the last goal that you set for yourself. Chances are that you either reached that goal or perhaps just under it, but have you ever over-achieved in reaching a goal? I haven't.

I believe that the goals we set for ourselves are usually the area where we will find ourselves. Richard Branson, Donald Trump and Tony Robbins all possess the same trait in setting big goals because they know they are only limited by their thinking and therefore they aim outrageously high.

If you feel insecure about your dreams then you can be assured that everyone else feels the same way. 99 percent of people don't believe they are able to achieve big goals and therefore aim for realistic and reasonable goals. The competition is therefore fiercest for the mediocre. The other 1% live in the top sphere completely untroubled, growing their goals in size as they see the benefit of doing so.

Don't overestimate the competition and under estimate yourself. If Tony Robbins could go from being a janitor to the world's most renowned inspirational speaker and multimillionaire then why can't you? If Eminem could go through all his adversity to inspire millions around the world with his profound lyrics then why can't you?

All of the famous and amazing people we see around us and hear about in the tabloids were just normal people like you and I at some stage. It was not as if Nelson Mandela was born the greatest leader that South Africa would ever know. He was born a baby and with goals and determination became the man he was destined to become. You are better than you think and you can achieve anything that you can dream up. We are only limited by the power of our minds.

Another reason for dreaming unrealistically and unreasonably is that it provides you with an adrenaline injection. Having a big dream with a large pay off will provide motivation to overcome the inevitable obstacles you will face whilst pursing your dream.

If I dream that I want to go to Cape Town for two extra days in December and my manager pushes back saying; "We need you for those two days Laurens, you can't take off work." I wouldn't fight back much, I would just think to myself; "Ag it's ok, it was only two extra days. I can always do that next year."

But if my dream is to sail across the ocean from the lush Cape Town paradise to the pristine white beaches and turquoise clear sea of the Greek Islands I will go through hell and high water to make it happen. "Sorry boss, I've got fifteen days of leave and I am taking all of them. This is a once in a lifetime experience that I will never forgive myself for not doing."

It makes sense, doesn't it? The bigger the dream, the more the payoff will be and therefore the greater the incentive to pursue that dream.

Imagine that you were the smartest, biggest and strongest person in the world with no limits. What would you want in your life? What would you dream to have in your life if you knew you could not fail? Write down the dreams that you come up, remembering that this process has no limits, don't judge how you will realise your dreams, jot them down and begin to enjoy the feelings that comes from liberating yourself from limits.

As you begin to write down your dreams match the previous dream with a bigger dream. For example if you were to write down I am going to travel to India, you can 'beat' that dream by saying; 'Why stop at India, let's travel around the entire Asian Continent'. Again it doesn't have to be realistic or even seem possible at the moment. If you look at your dreams and they begin to scare you then you are on the right track.

Wilbur and Orville Wright had to be unrealistic and unreasonable to get man to fly and guess what? They got it right. When they first came up with the idea they didn't know how it would come about they just began to dream. Once we begin to dream we begin to send out signals to the universe and the universe responds with the HOW to do it. "If you cannot see yourself as a winner, then you cannot perform as a winner." – Zig Ziglar

COVER ALL ASPECTS

Once you have gotten the hang of dreaming big from the previous section it is time to structure your thinking so that you cover every aspect of your life. Align each dream to the dimensions described below:

- Mental
- Physical
- Spiritual
- Social
- Work life

This structure can also help probe more thinking. If you have ten dreams in the mental space but only one in the social space then you can focus your thinking on your social sphere. If you really value your physical sphere, then you can add more dreams there. The structured thinking helps probe a well-rounded thought process.

Once you have the dreams written down, it's time to bring them back down to reality and turn them into actions that will result in the desired outcome.

SMART

Dreaming big is the first step to having the life you deserve. It's great that you have done the first part and now it's about action.

There is no difference between a pessimist and an optimist in denial. The pessimist says; 'There's no hope, so why bother doing anything?' The optimist in denial says; 'Don't worry about doing anything, it's going to turn out fine.' Either way nothing happens. We need to take a step into the right direction and begin putting in action what needs to be done in order to achieve that dream.

SMART is the generally accepted term for setting effective goals. The acronym is defined on the following page:

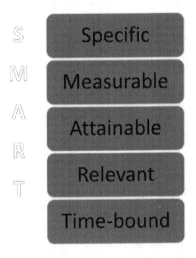

Think about a current goal that you have been wanting to achieve. It could be anything from making more money, to losing weight or even attracting the right person into your life. Once you have the goal in mind write down anything and everything that you can think of that will help you achieve your goal, called action items. The point is not to be critical but to let your hand and mind move freely into a non-judgemental creative zone and get down as many ideas as possible.

If you want to make more money for example the potential action items could be to work towards an increase at work, to invest in a passive income-generating asset or to reduce expenses... These ideas can be large, medium or small, they can be long-term or short-term, it doesn't really matter as long as the creative juices start flowing. Give yourself around fifteen minutes to complete this task.

Once you have your various action items that will help you achieve your goal put an asterisk next to those that are critical to achieving the goal, and that you can achieve within your current control. If one of your action items for earning more money is to become the CEO then that is maybe out of your control, though cutting down on your expenses is within your control.

This will immediately give you some direction and a sense of clarity. You will also be empowered because the goals you stipulate are ones that you have control over. We can now take the asterisked action items and turn them into SMART goals and create a clear plan forward.

SPECIFIC

What is the point of having a specific goal? I asked this question while watching one of my favourite movies, Alice in Wonderland. I love the movie for its wonder and excitement, though on this occasion the movie taught me about goal setting. Alice was at a cross roads and asked "Would you tell me, please, which way I ought to go from here?"

The cat replied, "That depends a good deal on where you want to get to."

"I don't much care where" – Alice said naively.

"Then it doesn't matter which way you go." –

The cat said. You will only get where you want to go, and if you don't know where that is how will you know that you have gotten there?

A specific goal is described as a goal that is clear and unambiguous, without vagaries and platitudes. For goals to be specific, they must detail why it's important, who's involved, where it's going to happen and which attributes will be needed.

Here are a few examples of very typical non-specific goals:

- I'm going to learn to do Latin dancing.
- I'm going to lose a lot of weight!
- I'm going to play better golf.
- I'm going to learn computer programming.
- I'm going to learn to play the piano.

You can hopefully see how useless these goals are because how would you ever know if you have reached the intended destination of the set goal? The lack of accurate goal setting sets us up for failure, disappointment and in turn will demotivate you to try again.

Let's take those same goals and make them success/ fail quantifiable specific goals; why it's important, who's involved, where it's going to happen and which attributes are important.

- I'm going to learn how to Cha-Cha at the dance studio around the corner. I know my wife will appreciate it and then I can show her how important she is to me.
- I'm going to lose 10 kilograms through the Weigh-Less support team. I need to maintain my health so that I can be the active dad my kids deserve.
- I'm going to improve my golf game through diligent weekly training with the head coach, Morne. I want to decrease my overall shots per game from 98 to 90. Golf is a crucial business sport and in order to grow my business I need to improve.
- I'm going to learn how to build a PHP form that takes a user's information and inserts it into a MySQL database. Computer programming is a hobby and it is important to be able to distract myself with things that interest me.
- I'm going to learn how to play 'Isn't She Lovely' by Stevie Wonder on the piano. I want to show my daughter how to play it because she wants to learn to play the piano but is scared it will be too difficult.

These are all success or fail goals.

- You can either complete a Cha Cha sequence or you can't.
- You either lost 10 kilograms or you didn't.
- You either reduced your shots from 98 to 90 or you didn't.
- You either built a PHP form and MySQL connection or you didn't.
- You either learned the song 'Isn't She Lovely' or you didn't.

At least from this point of view you can see whether you have achieved your goal or not and from there take the correct actions to achieve them.

Wikipedia defines a specific goal to incorporate the five 'W' questions below:

1. **What:** What do I want to accomplish?
2. **Why:** Specific reasons, purpose or benefits of accomplishing the goal.
3. **Who:** Who is involved?
4. **Where:** Identify a location.
5. **Which:** Identify requirements and constraints.

Use the specificity of the goal to motivate clear and unambiguous action to achieving that goal. "If you aim at nothing, you will hit every time!" – Zig Ziglar. Use the above questions to give a specificity to your goals.

MEASURABLE

One of my New Year's resolutions of 2010 was to play better golf. I had it on my vision board for the entire year and constantly studied it. Nearing the end of 2010 I reviewed the goals I had set on my vision board to see how much I had achieved.

I looked at my vision of playing better golf with a feeling of dismay. "I didn't achieve my goal." – I muttered in disappointment. I tore up the picture of Tiger Woods, which I used to symbolise better golf, and never went back to reinstating that goal. As I look back at it now I didn't give myself a measurable goal. In other words I would never know if I achieved the goal.

I didn't say I want to be playing with a five handicap. I didn't say that my average putting stroke should decrease from 2.5 per hole to 2 per hole. I didn't say I want my driving distance to increase by 10%. How would I know if I had reached my goal?

A measurable goal will usually answer questions such as:

1. How much?
2. How many?
3. How will I know when it is accomplished?
4. Can the indicators be quantified?

Ensure that you are setting a goal that can be measured. Being able to measure your goal will allow you to see how far you have come and where you could potentially improve. Let's say that my goal to improve my golf game was measurable in that I wanted to increase my driving distance by thirty metres.

I would probably be disappointed if I looked back at the end of 2010 and saw that my driving distance had increased by only twenty metres. Once the disappointment of missing the goal subsides I would be inspired by the fact that I am making progress; "I might not have achieved thirty metres, but at least I've gotten to twenty metres."

I can now revise my goal for the next year to say I want to achieve an extra ten metres, ultimately leading to the goal I desired. Setting a measurable goal keeps you focused on the achievement while small victories, like the twenty metres gain, provide motivation.

ATTAINABLE

I have always wanted to fly a helicopter. It has been a boyhood dream of mine since I could remember. I was seven years old when the dream first took hold. I asked my dad if he would take me to a helicopter place so that I could learn to fly. My dad hated to disappoint me but knew that you had to be a certain age before you would be allowed to learn to fly a helicopter.

My dad tried to make sense of my limitations in this short conversation; "Laurens, you know that you can be anything you want to be?" "Yes" – I naively replied. "Sometimes we can only get our dreams when God gives us permission. You have to be a little bit older before you can fly Laurens." "I can wait daddy. Maybe tomorrow God will give me permission." – I responded innocently. My dad smiled and said; "There is always a chance."

We have to wait for the right time in order to achieve a goal. If you want to be the President then you won't be able to achieve that dream within a few hours. Setting yourself an unattainable goal will demotivate you to try again. Instead of setting the goal of becoming President, you can set the goal of joining a Toastmaster's Club in order to practise the art of presentation which is crucial for a President role.

An achievable goal will usually answer the question:

1. How can the goal be accomplished?

RELEVANT

It was eight pm, Thursday evening the night before my final matric exam and I was ecstatic. My goal was not to study and pass my final exam but rather to party the night away after the exam. This obviously didn't motivate me to study much and therefore I didn't get the marks that I had wanted. We need to set relevant goals that will motivate us to achieve the next task in order to achieve the bigger goal.

The goal was not completely useless as I had motivation to finish my exam, but my motivation wasn't completely aligned to the goals that I wanted to achieve... being good marks. Sometimes we set great goals but they may not be relevant to what we are actually trying to achieve.

A relevant goal will positively answer these questions:

1. Does this seem worthwhile?
2. Is this the right time?
3. Does this match my other efforts or needs?
4. Am I the right person?
5. Is it applicable in the current socio, economic or technical environment?

TIME-BOUND

I want to learn to speak French... a goal that I have set for myself for many years and specifically for two reasons; firstly because it could help me further my career in certain countries of interest (African countries) and secondly because who doesn't love the awesome French 'le accent'.

I set this goal in the beginning of my high school career, a long long time ago. One of the reason that I have yet to achieve this goal is because I didn't put a time frame to it. There was no incentive or pressure for me to get on board with achieving the goal. I set the same goal, I want to learn French and this time set a time line to the goal.

I decided that I would begin with French classes before I travelled to France eight months later. Within two weeks I joined a French class as the incentive to get it done was there. It was not a dream anymore but rather a real objective that I could begin working on.

A time-bound goal will usually answer the question:

1. When?
2. What can I do six months from now?
3. What can I do six weeks from now?
4. What can I do today?

Take the action items that will result in your dream coming true and apply the SMART principle to them to ensure effective motivation to achieving your goals.

Here is a quick example of a non-SMART goal transformed into a SMART goal:

Not a SMART goal:

Employees will improve their writing skills.

This goal cannot be measured, has no time frame, nor any incentive as to why the improvement is needed or how it will be used.

A SMART goal:

The Department has identified a goal to improve communications among administrative staff by implementing an internal departmental newsletter. Elaine will complete a business writing course by January 2010 and will publish the first monthly newsletter by March 2010. Elaine will gather input and/or articles from others in the department and draft the newsletter for supervisor review, and after approval, will distribute the newsletter to staff by the 15th of each month.

The steps defined by Tony Robbins are simple and effective. Start with the result in mind as this helps overcome the inevitable trials and tribulations you will face with activities leading to a dead-end. Determine your why/purpose – which is going to serve as your motivator when things get tough. Dream big and create an action plan filled with SMART goals that will, through consistent hard work, result in your desired outcomes.

GET MOMENTUM

When Tony Robbins explained the concept of goal setting to me what stuck out the most was his focus on momentum. He always said; "Never leave a goal setting site without taking immediate action."

If you for example want to lose weight then an immediate action after setting the goal could be to go into the kitchen and throw away all the chocolate in the cupboard. It will help cure the disease of someday. It is a great tool to use to get the ball rolling, once it has started one can keep it going with less effort than the original push required.

It makes sense, doesn't it? Think about the second of January when you begin to set goals for the year ahead. How excited are you? The dreams look real and the motivation is high. The next day the motivation is a little less, and by the end of the month the goals are a distant memory hidden away in the back store room of the garage. Getting the ball rolling is the hardest part and therefore requires the most energy, and when is the motivation highest? When the goal is set.

Therefore it makes sense to start working towards achieving that goal once the goal has been set and the motivation is high. The power of momentum is immense. Think about when you start watching a series. Once you have gotten through the first episode it is so easy to go on to the next one. After three or so you are hooked on the story line and the day flashes past. Once you get comfortable on the couch it is easy to spend the day there, isn't it?

What is the hardest part about exercising? It's getting to the gym, isn't it? Once you are at the gym nothing stops you from exercising. I don't know anyone who has ever entered the gym and left because they didn't feel like it. They drove all the way from their houses to gym and they will make sure that their effort is not wasted.

Use momentum to your advantage. It is the hardest part to start, to get the ball rolling. Use the high excitement and motivation when setting the goal.

[See exercises for this chapter at the end of the book]

GETTING A PARTNER IN CRIME

I attended a Seminar at the end of 2013 with my close friend, Bradley. We had both been getting into the positive thinking habit. It seemed destined when we received a mail inviting us to join the seminar on creating wealth through positive thinking.

The presenter said that many times we set goals for ourselves that no one else knows about, then when times are tough and we don't think that we can achieve those goals we give up on them and sweep them under the rug. "No one else knew about the goal so it's not like I'm embarrassing myself." Isn't that true?

However when you tell all your friends and family that you are going to do something, regardless of the hardship, you are going to try until the bitter end. You have to save face, it is a part of our human survival need. When humans were still living in caves they were sent out to gather food, and if they came home empty-handed I don't think our ancestors would have accepted the fear of failure as a plausible excuse. Therefore when we tell other people about our dreams and goals we are likely to push ourselves more than if the dream is known only to ourselves.

It is important for you to choose a reliable friend, one that will be strict with you. If you confess your goals to him then he must be able to confront you at the deadline and ask about the result. It should be someone that you look up to and wouldn't want to let down. The stronger this connection and need to please the more motivating it will be for you to achieve your goals.

Bradley and I immediately saw value in the theory and began to confess like alcoholics who had been binging for weeks.

I told him about the first goal that came to mind which was to finish reading 'The Secret to Thinking Big' which I had started months prior but kept abandoning using the clichéd *'life getting in the way'* excuse. I told him that I wanted to finish reading the book by the end of the month, giving me exactly twenty days till the due date.

Hyped from the seminar we rushed off home and my motivation led me to read thirty-five pages... this goal was going to be easy to achieve I thought. A couple of days passed and I had completely forgotten about the said agreement.

I called Bradley three days before the due date with a fake cough; "Hey Brad *cough* ah man I'm feeling so down. *cough* I obviously couldn't finish the book, sorry man *cough*" He said it was ok, he understood and just like that we had fallen into the trap of *'its ok to not achieve your goals'*.

We had missed a crucial part of the *getting a partner in crime* principle which was to describe the painful punishment to follow the failure of a goal. Think about the time you were a kid and your homework needed to be done. In my home my mom was the first to approach me and say; "Laurens have you done your homework?" "No." – I would reply disinterestedly. "Well then you best get to it now!" – My mom would say sternly. An innocent smile would cross my face as I politely ignored her and carried on playing whatever game was interesting at that time.

Then when my dad got home he would ask the same question; "Laurens have you done your homework?" "No." – I would reply squeamishly. "If you do not start your homework now I'm getting the belt." – He would say angrily. Immediately I would drop everything I was doing and rush over to my room to diligently begin working on my homework. The pain of the punishment can drive the right motivation so why not harness that motivation to help drive the right behaviour you need in achieving your goals.

After Bradley and I revisited the comments from the seminar we began to add pain to the punishment of unfinished goals. I told Bradley; "Ok, I want to join a speaking club in order to practise the art of better communication and I want to join by the end of November." Bradley nodded in agreement and asked; "What's the punishment, brother?" I looked at him and reflected on something which would really motivate me.

Now you have to be honest with yourself in this situation. You could say that if I do not achieve this goal then I will go out with my friends to my favourite bar and have drinks till someone has to drive me home... but what behaviour is that driving? I collected my thoughts and answered; "If I don't join a club I have to wash my car, your car and your girlfriend's car... at twelve pm... in the blistering sun without clothes on."

It sounds a little extreme, doesn't it? And to be honest I don't think Bradley would have held me to it but again it's the motivation that counts. I remember on the 27th of November being on the phone to every Toastmasters Club in South Africa desperately looking for a membership position. By the end of November I had made a plan and joined a club within range, and more importantly I didn't need to do the full Monty whilst washing three cars in the blistering Africa sun.

Lastly it is important for you to choose a partner in crime who is going to hold you to your word. You know the person in your life who is not a complete walk over and who won't take 'no' for an answer. Quickly think about who that person is for you? Bradley was the perfect candidate for me as he is my best friend and iconic role model... he is the last person I would ever want to disappoint.

The art of this motivation technique is to be critical with yourself. You know who you are and what will motivate you best. Don't go to a shy friend of yours with a punishment that you know he will not insist on or that doesn't motivate the right behaviour.

Ask yourself the following questions to help harness the power of *saving face:*

1. What behaviour is required? – Calling multiple clubs to find out more information in order to make the decision and join a club
2. What motivation will drive that action? Something worse than calling many people, doing manual labour in the sun without clothes on sounds pretty terrible to me.
3. Which person will drive that motivation? Someone I respect and who respects me enough to stand his ground, knowing what is the best for me.

I hope you understand by now how to get motivated and setting achievable goals with the tools needed to get the ball rolling. I would quickly like to take you through a habit that I adopted using the tools and techniques described in this chapter.

THE HAPPINESS HABIT

One of my favourite TedxTalks of all time is 'The Happiness Advantage', by Shawn Achor, and I make reference to this quite often as it was instrumental in my growth and success this far. After his riveting talk about the science of happiness, which is backed up with years of psychological research, he defines five small lifestyle changes to ensure eternal happiness.

The five principles defined in that TedxTalk are:

1. Journaling – writing in your diary
2. Gratitude of 3
3. Conscious acts of kindness
4. Meditation
5. Physical Exercise

His authentic storytelling coupled with hard research mesmerised me to try the above five techniques. I made it my goal to practise the principles religiously for the twenty-one days that he recommended in making them a habit. Some of the principles took longer than the twenty-one days to become natural but within six months of hearing his presentation I am proud to say that each of the five principles form part of my daily routine... and it works. Happiness is not just found, it is worked at every single day.

Journaling

I instantly got the ball rolling by closing YouTube after the presentation and opening a word document titled; 'Laurens' Positive Journal'. I struggled at first to come up with at least one positive sentence, and finally after a bit of deep diving I wrote, '*I enjoyed the lunch I had with my sister*'. It wasn't a revolutionary sentence but at least a start. I sat for another five minutes sifting through my mind for a different positive experience but nothing came to mind. I wasn't too disappointed as at least I had started, and I am well aware that habits are not formed in a day.

Since that day I have opened up my computer every night before bed and for not more than five minutes jotted down a few positive things that happened to me during the day. The five minutes quickly turned to ten minutes and then fifteen minutes as writing the positive sentence sparked a positive mood within me and I was able to see more positives than I could ever before. Shawn had explained in his talk that through journaling you allow your mind to relive the positive experience and I was a happy recipient of that feeling.

The goal I have defined for myself now is to write a minimum of five positive sentences per day. (SMART)

GRATITUDE OF 3

My usual morning ritual was to drowsily open the taps for the shower and stand in despair dreading work and keeping the thought of the imminent weekend as my only salvation. After watching Shawn I decided to enhance my shower experience to include a short conversation with myself about three things that I am grateful for in my life. I already had the habit of showering every morning, and now I packaged the gratitude habit into that routine – expending no extra time on my morning ritual.

At first, like with the journaling, the positive thoughts were far and few between. I started by forcing gratitude and feeling like a bit of a deceitful idiot. I motivated myself to keep going by telling Julie about my goal. I forced the strange feelings into submission, as my ego was on the line and again like the journaling the five minute shower became too short because I had so many positive things to be grateful for; things like my family, that I have a job in the current economic climate, the security of a home and food every day, and that I have another day to live...

The goal I have defined for myself now is to be grateful for a minimum of three things per day. (SMART)

The above two habits in total took less than fifteen minutes of my day and I literally began to see the results in one week. The journaling allowed me to relive my positive experience and when a day seemed full of negativity I would go to my previous day's journal and get motivation that good things are in my life. The gratitude of three was a simple two minute process included into my showering routine where I reminded myself that I am blessed and highly favoured.

This constant reminder of positivity allowed me to recap the good things I experience in my life every day. Whenever I felt the unease of boredom, lack of interest or irritation fill my body my mind immediately triggered the thought; "What can I be grateful for?" I was able to see things that I had never before seen. I was constantly focusing on reasons to be happy and fulfilled and as the old saying goes… 'Ask and you shall receive!'

Before I started this seemingly far-fetched fifteen minute habit, which I was very sceptical of at first, my mind was filled with worry and despair and I was able to find more reasons to be upset than happy in my every day environment. My focus was on the despair and as mentioned what you focus on the longest becomes the strongest. Focusing on a good habit manifests it into your reality and you will enjoy the benefits.

Now when I find myself in a boring and useless meeting, instead of taking that as reality I will create a hype about it by looking at the possibilities of fun and success within the meeting. I wouldn't say to myself; 'Ag, what a waste, this meeting has no value' because then my time felted wasted. I would rather say; 'I'm so lucky to have a job, I can learn something new in this meeting and I could even form a valuable relationship with some of the people in the meeting'. Then my time felt like it was being put to good use and my positive emotion rubbed off on everyone and my ability to constantly make a good impression went through the roof.

The next three habits took slightly longer to become part of my life.

Conscious acts of kindness

I began a project on my Facebook page called #1000ActsOfKindness where I wanted to complete 1000 kind acts within a year and a half. The purpose behind this habit was powerful, I wanted to inspire my audience to become more generous and to show that one person can make a difference in the hope that my audience would feel empowered to make a difference in the world.

In South Africa you constantly see piles of rubbish lying around and people in need of all kinds of help, though before starting the project I didn't have enough motivation to pick up the rubbish or help the needy. Once I had this project up and running I had a reason and a purpose for picking up the rubbish. My Purpose compelled me to overcome the feelings of lethargy.

The more I gave the more I realised how much I have. I added to the already present abundant mind-set that I had achieved with the previous two habits. I got momentum with the project and the twenty one days of consecutive acts had ingrained kindness into my routine. I incorporate the habit of abundance in my life, appreciating what I have and reminding myself how much I have by giving to the less fortunate.

The critical success factor to incorporating this habit was twofold. One was using a powerful purpose to drive motivation in the tough times and second I told my entire Facebook following about my goal and the 'saving face' factor ensured consistent action.

The goal I have defined for myself now is to complete three acts of kindness per day, which will ensure that I reach the #1000ActsOfKindness within the allotted time. (SMART)

Meditation and physical exercise

The last two habits that Shawn recommends came through conscious effort and scheduling. I would sit with my diary on Sunday evenings to plan out the week and its objectives. I would immediately schedule an evening for Yoga and another evening for meditation. It formed part of my MAP. It's as Tony Robbins says; "Plan it and it becomes something, schedule it and it becomes reality."

A few months later and now I'm doing yoga and meditation every morning before work and every evening before bed. The spiritual advantages of doing meditation and yoga far surpass the effort to do them. I can immediately feel it when I have not done yoga before work as my emotions are out of balance and my energy levels are way down.

All of these simple habits are now a part of me to the point where not doing them feels more uncomfortable than doing them. It takes a little to mean a lot, it's the little things you do every day that makes the difference, to build the habit and by doing so change your life.

It's what we do every day that makes the difference. Start small. Start with today and make today count. Move to tomorrow with the momentum of changing the only thing you have conscious control over... the NOW. Keep making every day a new day to make your dream come true, to reach your goals and enjoy the twenty-one day journey where you transform your life into the one that you know you deserve. Work on small goals every day and your life will transform.

It takes a little bit of effort every day to be happy, positive and getting into the right psychology, the right frame of mind. As you begin to adopt the continuous actions to change they will become automatic, like the washing process. It is up to you to make the change happen.

CHAPTER 5

IT'S UP TO YOU

What you think about is what you become. Our thoughts are the cornerstone of our being and they manifest into reality to make us who we are. It is solely our thoughts and actions that produce our reality. While others have the ability to influence our thoughts we must ultimately decide which thought we wish to act on.

I know it seems easier said than done, but we have to first give consent to other people to impart feelings of despair into our moods with their actions. I had a friend, Simon, who on matric holiday, felt pressured to try drinking and driving. He said that everyone around him was doing it and he felt at times that it's not as dangerous as he once thought.

Simon's mom always built up the fear of drinking and driving, reiterating that one mistake could be fatal. And lucky this persuaded him not to drink and drive that night. However, seeing his friends doing it made it seem less dangerous than he once thought. Their actions began to manipulate his thoughts slightly.

Simon withstood the pressure and called his mom to get assurance from her; "They won't stop harassing me about drinking, mom." – He said nervously. Naturally she was very proud of how he handled the situation and quickly jumped into action to get him away from the negative influence in his life.

Simon's thoughts were being infected by other people's actions but he still had the final decision, the final say. His friends made drinking and driving seem like it was not fatal or even dangerous as his mom always advised. This influence nearly convinced him to try.

I'm thankful that Simon made the final decision to say no and that he stuck with what he believed was true. It is empowering to think that we are in control of our destiny. We are the authors and directors of our own story and once you accept that your life is UP TO YOU and no one else but you, you can take charge and make things happen.

BEER FEST REVELATION

One limiting belief that has frequently arisen in my short journey of coaching people is; "Other people bring me down." "Everyone makes me feel worthless." Everyone saying the same thing in a different way; that they are not in control of their destiny. We often feel that people are out to get us, right? That they will stop at nothing to bring us down.

I was at the Beer Fest in South Africa at Monte Casino at the end of October celebrating my soon to be brother-in-law, Steph's, bachelor party. He was dressed in a tiger onesie and needless to say captured the imagination and attention of almost everyone at the beer fest.

While gallivanting around using Steph as an ice-breaker I met a lot of interesting people and the most interesting were at the bachelorette party taking place at the next table. As is customary we began the conversation using the common ground of 'losing' a friend to the opposite sex to initiate interest. I met a girl named Claire who had done a lot of meditating, something that I am very interested in, and we immediately connected.

For over twenty minutes we went into a high intensity debate on the positive effects of meditation and how we had gotten into the routine. It felt as if we were alone at the Beer Fest, completely absorbed by the *not so common* interest that we had in meditation.

At the twenty minute mark in the conversation she asked; "Sorry, but I don't even know your name?" It was quite a light-hearted moment as we both reflected on how absorbed we had been in the interesting debate that we hadn't even had time to exchange names.

Through our brief introduction one of Claire's friends joined the conversation, and it wasn't long until we engaged in the high speed examination of meditation. Claire's friend, who had just joined, didn't quite have the same interest in meditation Claire and I shared and so quickly felt left out. She looked angrily over at me and said; "Why are you guys just ignoring me?"

This girl was at least thirty years old and I thought surely she can't be that insecure thinking that we were ignoring her. She walked away from our conversation in a huff, I looked over at Claire to reassure her that I was not trying to be rude. Claire smiled at me and replied; "I know, she just makes everything about her." Claire and I blissfully carried on with our conversation.

The next day I looked back at that situation and it resonated with me. Her friend joined our conversation and thought that we were completely ignoring her when in actual fact we were just indulging in a mutually interesting topic. Her friend, like many of us, made everything about herself... and that's not a bad thing because at the end of the day she has to look out for herself. She is in charge of her life and therefore must consider what is best for her, right?

Understanding that no one else really has our best interest at heart should reinforce the fact that if you want to live the life of your dreams it is up to you. You have the power to take action and create your life according to your vision. I'm not saying you must kick everyone out of your life so that you can selfishly follow your dream, as it is imperative that you have a support system and a foundation on which to pursue your happiness. Others can help and guide you but you must make it happen.

Other people around you will not always see your potential, your dreams and therefore you must see it for yourself. You must know that if you want a better life, IT IS UP TO YOU. Others can influence you but you are in control, you make the decisions and your destiny is based solely on your actions. Simon was tempted by the actions of the people around him but he focused on what he believed in and what his mom had taught him. It was what he focused on that became the priority and helped him make the right decision and take charge of his life.

WHAT YOU FOCUS ON THE LONGEST BECOMES THE STRONGEST

Look around the room quickly. Count the number of red objects that you can see. Do you have the number of red objects? Now without looking again how many objects in the room are blue? Obviously you would have no idea because you were looking for red objects.

Now if you look around for all the blue objects I am sure you will find many. You might even find objects that aren't blue, they're actually turquoise but you will count them anyway. The point is what you look for is what you will find. If you look for any reason to be happy right now, could you find one? This is the crucial question to ask if you want a series of happy days.

We can choose a specific beneficial perspective to focus on dependent on our needs; i.e. do we want to see the cell phone as an alarm clock or a calculator? Using focus you can take your attention and energy to a specific point in reality. If we are focusing on everything that we don't have that is all we will see. We will see that we don't have enough money, enough friends, and enough opportunities and eventually we will become victims in our story.

The opposite is also true, if we focus on everything we already have we will have enough and more. We will see that we are blessed to have enough money to live, enough friends to be satisfied and a vast amount of opportunities every day.

This concept is based on the book 'The Secret', by Rhonda Byrne, which speaks about the law of attraction and that your attitude either brings more into your life or takes more away. The attitude of gratitude, focusing on what you want, is the key to having enough and attracting more into your life.

My best friend Brad went through a tough time when one of his closest friends became an acquaintance. Brad is an extremely caring guy, which is one of my favourite characteristics, and he really didn't take it well when the friend he once called a brother pretty much deserted him. Brad went through a stage of despair trying to reconnect with his old friend but alas he wanted nothing more to do with Brad.

A month after the horrendous experience I invited Brad over for a chat, I was sure he needed some support. He entered the room smiling from ear to ear as if happiness had just crashed into his car. "And now?" – I asked with enthusiastic excitement. "Oh nothing really, I'm just happy to be here hanging out with my best friend." – Brad said. I was overwhelmed by the compliment as well as his attitude towards the destructive experience he had just been through.

"Thing is Laurens, I've maybe lost a friend but I'm grateful to still have a great one here." – He said, smiling in my direction. I was so impressed with Brad. He had gone through a tough time but instead of focusing on the heartache he was able to change his focus to something that made him feel good again.

Our friendship since has never been stronger as he values me more in his life every day. With this new vision he now has more time to be with the friends that want to be around him and he gets more satisfaction than ever before.

Every situation can be seen from different perspectives. Some are helpful and some aren't, but it will forever always be up to us to decide which we want to use. With some of my clients that I coach I see a lot of focus and energy going into things they cannot change. They will worry about what the weather will be like, how their managers will treat them and what the economy is going to do next. The question

I always have for them, is; "Will focusing on that help you achieve what you want to achieve?"

The answer is always the same... NO.

Placing your focus and expending energy on things you cannot change is a waste of your time. Watching the news is, in my opinion, more destructive than helpful as it puts you into a mood of fear without anyway of changing that fear. I like to inspire my clients to shift their focus and energy from what they cannot change to what they have full control over... their actions.

MR KELVIN

At University I had a tough subject, Artificial Intelligence, and I was hovering around the failure mark. It was undoubtedly the most difficult subject of my entire four year Computer Science Degree. I approached the Artificial Intelligence lecturer, Mr Kelvin, and begged for mentoring on the subject; "I just don't understand what is going on, Sir. Could I please steal an hour of your week for the rest of the semester to make sure I conquer this subject?" To which Mr Kelvin kindly agreed.

I entered Mr Kelvin's office the next Tuesday morning ready for the first session. Once the brief introductions were concluded Mr Kelvin asked me; "What do you expect from these sessions?" I looked at him in puzzlement; "Uhm, I'm hoping to get motivation to study and pass this subject." – I replied. Mr Kelvin smiled and replied; "Good answer, let's begin, shall we?"

Over the brief sixty minute sessions that Mr Kelvin and I engaged in I learnt a lot about Artificial Intelligence concepts but also a lot about self-motivation and empowerment. He had a keen passion for computers but unknown to us, an immense passion of his was developing young people across the social spectrum.

Mr Kelvin was only thirty years old and was able to relate to our generation far more effectively than some of the other fossils torturing us by reading line by line from the text book.

A month passed and my understanding of Artificial Intelligence had definitely improved and Mr Kelvin was impressed. He decided that I had put in a lot of effort and that he wanted to push me to not just passing the subject but thriving... "Laurens, it's been a month and I'm happy with your progress. I want to challenge you, try attempt the exercise at the end of Chapter three by yourself and bring it to my office at our next meeting, ok?" – Mr Kelvin politely asked. "Of course, Sir. I'm happy to do it." – I replied.

The week flew past and suddenly it was thirty minutes before the meeting with Mr Kelvin. The work he had asked me to prepare would take well over two hours to complete and unfortunately my student life had taken priority.

I arrived at Mr Kelvin's office with my tail between my legs! He graciously opened the door and requested the work before entering. I looked down and mumbled; "I haven't finished it." Mr Kelvin paused briefly and while closing the door on me said; "See you next week then Laurens."

I was taken aback as I didn't expected that he would react in that manner. The whole point of the mentoring was to explain concepts, not to do extra work. However, after giving it some thought, I went home and dedicated two hours to completing the task to the best of my ability.

Mr Kelvin had courteously taken me under his wing and shared his knowledge freely with me so I thought giving my best would be the least I could do in return. The next week I arrived at Mr Kelvin's office with work in hand. Again he graciously opened the door and requested the work to which I happily responded with a written paper.

Mr Kelvin sat me down and immediately apologised for the way in which he treated me the week before; "Sorry for slamming the door in your face Laurens." – He began. "Please understand that I was trying to teach you a lesson. If you do not complete the work I give you then how do you expect me to give you the time of day?" To which I supportively nodded.

"The same thing will happen in life, if you do not put in the work then you cannot expect life to open up for you. If you do not work at your dream, work on building yourself up, engage the right networks, learning your product, and understand your environment then life is just going to slam the door right in your face. You must bring the work to the party and the doors will open up." – Mr Kelvin preached.

I sat contemplating what he had said. What a valuable life lesson indeed. We often expect life to work for us. The Lotto should go our way, my manager must give me a promotion and my dream must come true because I want it to. In reality we are not often willing to put in the hours to guarantee success.

Through my work with Mr Kelvin he taught me that I have to put in the work and success will be guaranteed. I have to study, complete assignments and teach myself the concepts... he was guiding me along the way but it was up to ME to get the work done.

I ended up getting a distinction for Artificial Intelligence and it was my highest mark on my report card. Mr Kelvin, congratulating my efforts, grabbed me aside whilst I was leaving his class for the last time; "Well done Laurens, you put in the work and you got the results." "Thank you for your support, Sir." – I said with genuine appreciation as he had taught me not only what Artificial Intelligence is but how to empower myself. He equipped me with the knowledge that my actions produced my results and that I had to take charge of my own life.

A lot of people come to me saying that they want the results that other people have but they are not willing to put in the time and effort that the others put in to get there. They want better jobs, bigger salaries and more appreciation from their managers but none of them do anything about it. They happily complain and wallow in their despair of how unfair life is. What they don't understand is that the person who is getting the better job, bigger salary and appreciation galore takes charge and works towards attaining that goal, he doesn't just find excuses to complain about it.

Instead of just complaining, determine the life you want to live and start to act accordingly. Complaining is like a rocking chair, it gives us something to do but it doesn't get us anywhere.

HILARY, THE ONLINE CRIMINAL

"Yes mom, they said yes." – I shrieked running into my mom's warm embrace. "The company said I could move to America next year for six months. Things are happening, mom." – I said in complete delight. I had finally been rewarded for all my hours of Toastmasters, coaching and working on myself that the company saw value enough in me to send me abroad to begin my adventures as the company's spokesperson.

My delight swiftly morphed into project management mode as I needed to ensure everything was organised before my impending trip overseas. I quickly drove home, whilst spreading the good news to my family, and as I entered our apartment I saw belongings that needed a new home. "My fridge has to go, my TV has to go and even my toaster has to go." – I said with little remorse, I knew that I would quickly find comfort in new possessions overseas.

I dashed to get my camera, took all the photos needed to showcase my stuff and immediately put it onto various online trading websites; OLX, GumTree, etc. All of my belongings were in perfect condition, as I had bought them only months prior, and were selling like hot cakes. I had put up an advert for my TV and within two minutes I had already received three calls about it.

Being a reasonable gentlemen I told all the prospective clients that whoever places money in my bank account is the lucky recipient of the brand new LED Samsung TV. A guy by the name of Hilary pounced on my offer and within fifteen minutes of our conversation he sent a cheque of R5000,-. Now if you know anything about money then you know that cheques are obsolete, dangerous and a general NO GO. Well guess what, I didn't know that!

My automatic trusting nature kicked in as I gave him the directions to my house. He swiftly picked up the TV and off he went... both of us seemingly satisfied. Six days later the penny dropped and the cheque bounced. My immediate reaction was to call Hilary and ask if something went wrong on his side, to which he responded; "I'm on my way to the bank now and I'll call you afterwards."

A few hours passed and I called him again; "Sorry to bother Hilary, but have you spoken to your bank?" To which he replied yet again that he was on his way and he'll call me afterwards. I sat in comfort thinking Hilary was a genuine good guy who had mistakenly given me a cheque that bounced.

A day later and multiple ignored calls, I became suspicious. I spoke to my sister about the event and as soon as I mentioned a cheque transaction her response was instant; "Have you given him the goods already Laurens?" "Yes, last week. Why?" – I asked naively.

Julie exhaled heavily on the line as she didn't want to give me the bad news; "I'm sorry Laurens, you've been scammed. The money and the TV are gone." I sat in quiet desperation contemplating how it was possible. Julie went on to explain the entire scam to me and I felt like a complete idiot. I tried desperately calling Hilary but with no success.

Everyone at work heard about the situation and gave me their condolences, each with their own experience of the scamming world; "It happens to all of us at some point." – They assured me. A week passed but my feelings of anger, despair and distraction didn't; "Why did this have to happen to me?" – I kept asking the higher powers. "I've done nothing wrong, I'm just trying to make a life for myself. I'm not trying to hurt anyone, or steal from them. Why did this have to happen to me?"

On my way to my mentor's office, Bax, I walked past a mirror and in disgust looked at myself as if to say; "What an idiot, you deserved this." With my tail between my legs and shoulders drooping heavily I entered Bax's pristine executive office. "What's wrong Laurens?" – Bax asked concernedly, he had never seen me so down in the entire two years that we had known each other.

I told him the story of exactly what had happened and after forty-five of the sixty allocated minutes I was still moaning about my bad luck. Finally I reached the end of a depressing saga and Bax said; "I'm sorry Laurens, this unfortunately happens to a lot of people... it's not your fault. Tell me, what are you going to do now?"

I sighed heavily and said; "Nothing really, there's nothing I can do right. Life's just against me at the moment." I was about to open my mouth to complain again when Bax reiterated his question; "What are you going to do now?" I thought maybe he hadn't heard me; "Nothing Bax I've just got bad luck, I can't do anything about it." Bax looked down disappointed; "I understand that you are down Laurens, but hasn't Hilary taken enough from you? Does he deserve your happiness too?" Anger filled my heart as I barked back immediately; "NO!"

"What are you going to do about it then Laurens?" – He asked again. "Maybe I can focus on my work to try forget about it?" – I asked unsure if that was the answer he was waiting for. "That's better Laurens." – He said cheerfully. "I don't mean to be hard on you but I want you to leave my office more empowered than when you walked in. Crying over spilt milk does not clean it up, does it?" – He wisely added. "No it doesn't." – I replied.

Bax used the rest of the sixty minute meeting reassuring me that complaining about my situation doesn't make it right, make me feel better or bring back my TV. Only my actions could change the way I feel. If I were to focus my energy on my work perhaps the feelings of inadequacy would lessen as my attention wouldn't be consumed with the mistake I had made but rather with the progress I was making at work.

Bax helped me realise that my actions are powerful but my complaints hold me in neutral. I cannot do anything about the scam artist but learn a lesson from the experience and move on stronger and wiser for it. The longer I focus on the fact that I got scammed and that I am helpless the more it erodes my self-confidence.

"Crying over spilt milk does not clean it up." You can be sad and down for a little while after a disappointment but don't stay there too long. Get back up and fight, because life is fraught with failure and getting back up is the key to success. Use these minor disappointments and see them as lessons learnt.

My lesson of knowing how cheques work was a R5000,- lesson and you can bet that I will NEVER let anyone pull the wool over my eyes in that regard again... R5000,- well spent in my books. Use action to get through these little disappointments that are going to inevitably make their way onto your path of success.

Success is a series of disappointments coupled with achievements and seeing that success doesn't happen overnight one might as well get use to facing inevitable disappointments along the way.

SUCCESS HAPPENS OVERNIGHT RIGHT?

When I was just fourteen years old and my sister's eighteen and twenty years old respectively, we spent a lot of time together watching movies. One of our favourite pastimes was to go to the cinema and choose a movie based on the cover only and nothing else. "I Am Legend" was showing and we unanimously decided to watch that that movie, mainly because we had heard such great things about it but also because Will Smith is the most talented actor ever.

After watching another Will Smith genius movie we began as always to debate the movie's meaning and how we had experienced it. I sat in the back seat as my sisters completely absorbed themselves in the debate of who Will Smith would choose if they both met him, which was a discussion that I had no part in. I sighed gloomily in the back of the car and said out loud; "Will Smith is so lucky. He has the coolest job, more money than he could ever need and ever girl loves him. He is so lucky."

Katherine, hearing my ramblings, broke away from the intense Mrs Smith debate to engage with me over my last statement. "He is lucky Laurens, you're right. Remember though that he didn't fall into fame and success. He worked really hard for it. He spent years building a rapping career before the opportunity to become an actor opened up. If he had decided to take the safe route and study, his rapping career would never have led to his acting roles." – Katherine explained

While Katherine broadened my horizon of Will Smith's background I tended to agreeing with her. I had just assumed that Will Smith was famous and rich because he had experienced more luck in his life and if I had his luck then I would be in his position. It was an unconscious limitation that I was placing upon myself. I surrendered to being the victim of my story by saying Will Smith was just at the right place at the right time and he was lucky to reach his goal.

Luck, by its definition, is unique and different to every person. If I say that because of Will's luck he is successful I immediately put him onto a pedestal and cut myself off at the knees. By thinking luck determines fate I restrict myself to a lower playing field where only my luck determines where my life goes.

We see Donald Trump as the property Guru of the world but before he struck it rich he went bankrupt four times. Would you have stopped after the first bankruptcy? I know I would. Colonel Sanders, the genius behind the KFC recipe, got rejected by over 1000 fast food chicken joints before someone bought his recipe. Thomas Edison, the inventor of the light bulb, founded 10 000 ways on how to not make a light bulb. In each of these cases success was preceded by multiple failures and determination to continue.

What we perceive is that success is overnight but what we fail to see is the hundreds and thousands of hours, failures and obstacles that these successful people have had to endure before they tipped the scale to become enormously successful. It is the work they put into following their dream every day that propelled them past the mere average. If we practise every day we will surely enter the winner's circle.

These titans of industry are not limited by the thoughts of people around them. They focus on what they can control, ensuring their actions are aligned to achieving ambitious results. They all realise that success is not a one hit wonder.

Gary Player, a former professional South African golf player and considered one of Golf Greats, famously said; "The more I play, the luckier I get." Think about it – the more I play the luckier I get – in other words the more I work at it the better I become and the more success I have. Gary and others put their heads down and grind away every day to improve their game. They know that the true secret of self-motivation is to engage in patient and consistent action.

IT TAKES PATIENCE AND CONSISTENT ACTION

There is a tree in the Far East that is known as the Chinese Bamboo tree. This tree has an extremely tough exterior and it takes five years of diligent nurturing, watering and sunlight in order for the tree to pierce the ground. Therefore the first five years of the tree's life is lived under the ground.

If one day of nurturing is missed the tree has a good chance of dying and collapsing in the ground. After five years of meticulously cultivating the tree it will finally penetrate the ground with a tiny shoot and just six weeks later the tree will have grown over 90ft tall.

Now the question is, did the tree take six weeks or over five years to grow 90ft tall? That's easy, it took over five years, because if at any time the person stopped watering, feeding and nurturing the tree, that tree would've died in the ground.

It's the same with your dreams, you'll be working hard at making them come true and the results won't be instant. People will laugh at you and ask you; "Why are you wasting your time watering your dream?" They may even mock you; "It's taken five years and you haven't even broken through the ground yet." Most people stop following their dreams because they don't get instant results, and consequently believe they have failed.

If you want something badly enough you have to keep watering your dreams. You have to create the foundation, the roots to support your 90ft growth. You have to nurture your dreams; you have to grow into the person who can achieve your dreams, learn the content to be an expert, practise your ability to perfection, create the right networks and when you encounter failure you have to get back up and keep believing and nurturing your dream. Every day we have to get back up to keep running towards our dream.

Once you have nurtured your dream enough you will break through the ground and begin to reap the benefits of the years of effort in creating the foundation. You will grow to 90ft in six weeks and the foundation you have built will be strong enough to support you.

If you had to become famous now because you built the first flying car but hadn't nurtured the knowledge on how to build it you might grow 90ft but your credibility, your foundation will be rocky and ultimately you would battle to sustain your height and would collapse.

To make your dream come true takes a lot of work, but that is work that we are capable of. We might not see the results instantly, our families may not believe us from the get go, but as we nurture our dreams they will begin to develop and our belief and confidence will grow.

Eventually we would have built the foundation and reaped the benefits of becoming the right person to make that dream a reality. We have to take control into our own hands. No one else is going to nurture our dream for us, it is OUR responsibility and OUR destiny.

Not everyone is going to see it for you, they will also not always want to help you reach your dreams. People are going to laugh but you have to remember that it is your dream and you're right to pursue it. You have to know that if you want to make your dream a reality then ITS UP TO YOU! You are the only one who take the prescribed medicine.

As Will Smith said in the movie 'The pursuit of happiness', "Don't ever let someone tell you that you cannot do something. You got a dream you gotta protect it. When people can't do something themselves they're gonna tell you that you can't do it. You want something, go get it. Period."

It is solely up to you to make your life the way you want it to be. Others will have their opinions but only you can act on what you believe and achieve what you set your mind to. Do you want change? Go out and GET IT. PERIOD.

My favourite passages of Les Brown goes as follows;

"People ask me, what do you do during the hard times Les? How do you get through them? My answer is always the same. You have to have faith! Faith is to call forth those things that are not as though they were. Judge not according to appearances, don't judge your circumstances and the possibilities of your future based upon what you have now and because of the challenges you are facing now. That's not the real reality. If you are going through some hard times, it has not come to stay it has come to pass. No matter how bad it is or how bad it gets... I am going to make it!"

Take charge of your life and go into the direction of your dreams.

Exercises

BECOMING SELF-AWARE (THE GAME)

This exercise is the corner stone of the entire book. Until we know where the cracks in the ceiling of our thoughts are, we are unable to make any positive progress towards replacing them with empowering thoughts. All the tools described in the later chapters will be rendered ineffective if one doesn't grasp the concept of self-awareness.

As explained above "The Game" is a quick trigger we can use to practise the art of awareness. Imagine that you are playing a game for the next five days and the game is called "The Game". Whenever you think of "The Game" or the "The Game" crosses your mind you must stop what you are doing and just listening to your thoughts.

If you are sitting at home watching some TV and your ad rushes into the room screaming with delight; "We won our golf game!" Game in the sentence could trigger you to remember "The Game" and before listening to the result of your ad's victory you can quickly listen to your thoughts.

Its sounds very simple right? The cool thing is that self-awareness is that simple, it is listening to the thoughts that are running through your mind and how these thoughts manifest in reality. For example if I have the thought of discomfort or anger then my body will react with folding my arms and turning away from the situation.

"The Game"

For the following five days try keep record of your progress with "The Game" technique.

Day One

Thought	Emotion
1.	
2.	
3.	
4.	

Day Two

Thought	Emotion
1.	
2.	
3.	
4.	

Day Three

Thought	Emotion
1.	
2.	
3.	
4.	

Day Four

Thought	Emotion
1.	
2.	
3.	
4.	

Day Five

Thought	Emotion
1.	
2.	
3.	
4.	

The trick of this exercise is to see what thought evokes what emotion. Is it the emotion that is empowering the right action or not?

THE HELPFUL QUESTION

"Ask and you shall receive."

Our minds are amazing organs. When we ask it a question, no matter how ridiculous the mind will come up with an answer. If we ask ourselves a lousy question, our minds will respond with a lousy answer.

Below is a serious of unhelpful questions which led your mind to answer in an unhelpful way.

Question	Mind Response
"Why does this always happen to me?"	"Because you deserve it!"
"Why can't a lose weight?"	"Because you're a pig."
"Why am I not motivated?"	"Because nothing I do matters?"

Below is a series of helpful questions with helpful responses from your mind.

Question	Mind Response
"Is it helpful?" or "What else could this mean?"	"No, so why think about it?" or "It could be a lesson"
"How could I exercise more?"	"Yes, mornings are open."
"What could motivate me right now?"	"Financial independence."

"The quality of your life is determined by the quality of your communication with yourself" – Tony Robbins.

Once you have mastered "The Game" it is critical that you do not judge the thoughts that cross your mind but rather try understand them. "Is it helpful?" is a non-judgemental way to dig deeper into your thoughts and find that value within them.

Take 5 thoughts, that you would like to understand better, from the previous exercise and ask yourself was it helpful in the moment? If the answer is yes, that's great. If the answer was no ask yourself if there was a more helpful thought that could've motivate the right behaviour in that situation.

Thought	Is It Helpful	Replacement Thought
Example: "Why does this always happen to me?"	No	"What reason could there be for me going through this situation?"
1.		
2.		
3.		
4.		
5.		

PERSPECTIVE EXERCISES

1. OPPORTUNITY GAGING QUESTIONING

Take a current challenging situation that you are experiencing and filter it through the following questions;

1. If I could see this situation as an opportunity what would that opportunity be?

_____

_____

_____

_____

2. Could I potentially learn a lesson through this challenge?

_____

_____

_____

_____

3. If I am successful in combating this challenge what would the result look like?

_____

_____

_____

_____

4. If I were to fail in combating this challenge what would the result look like?

_____

_____

_____

_____

Question one and two open your mind up to coming up with productive answers to inspire motivation and action. If we are looking for reasons why the challenge is insurmountable we will certainly find. The same applies with attempting to find reasons why the challenge is possible to overcome, if we look for them we will find them.

Question three and four help put the situation into a more realistic perspective. Nine times out of ten we will build up the fear like the Pit-Bull situation and running through the potential outcomes helps reduce the fears to a beatable Jack Russell.

When you are able to see any challenge as an opportunity to learn, grow and develop nothing will scare you anymore. Nothing will get in your way and stop you from realising your greatness. Remember that every challenge is just an opportunity in disguise.

2. Putting on new shoes

Take a current situation you are having a fight or argument with a friend or loved one and filter it through the following questions;

   1.   Why you are right? How did they make a mistake?

   _____
   _____
   _____
   _____

   2.   Why they are right? How did they perceive the scenario? What inconvenience did it cause them? Etc.

   _____
   _____
   _____
   _____

3. View the scenario from a third party perspective that has no prejudice. How would they see the scenario? How could both parties be right?

_____

_____

_____

_____

4. Is the argument worth losing the friend/loved one?

_____

_____

_____

_____

The point of this exercise is not to figure out with certainty that you are right and that the other person is wrong, it is more to allow yourself to see why that person reacted in that way and once understood and if the relationship is important you can be the bigger person and apologise.

This concept of visualising the situation from different perspectives is based on a Neuro-Linguistic Programming method called meta-mirroring. Meta-mirroring is to step back and see the problem in a new and perhaps more beneficial light.

The next time that you are in a hole with someone or an argument is brewing out of control ask yourself what they are seeing? Why they are upset? Often you will see something small that will help you rationalise their behaviour and if the person is important to you then you can create the motivation to apologise and stop the fire from spreading.

The power of putting yourself into another person's shoes is that you can get a completely different view on the situation at hand. For example take the following made-up scenario and view it from two lenses, the one lens of your favourite partying friend and the other lens of your mom.

It is the day before your final year exam, something that you have been working towards for four years and that your parents have attentively saved for since you were in nappies. Nine pm rears its head as you are way behind schedule, "looks like it's going to be another all-nighter" – you think to yourself.

A friend of yours phones you up and says there is a party of a lifetime around the corner, and he tries to convince to come for *just* one hour. Your pen hurriedly drops to the floor and off you go on a drinking binge. When the clock strikes three am your key finally enters the front door, you stumble in drunk as a skunk and completely un-phased about studying.

How would you mom perceive this situation compared to your friend? It doesn't take a genius to realise that your mom would be utmost disappointed where your friend would be utmost proud. It is the same situation but viewed through different people's lenses turns the reality upside down.

The power is with us to choose the most beneficial perspective to achieving our goals.

3. Looking long term

Take a current situation where you have embarrassed yourself and filter it through the following questions;

1. When will you no longer be embarrassed by the situation? (be it days, weeks, months or years)

_____
_____
_____
_____

2. Is it worth worrying about now? Are there other things you could be focusing on that would be more worth your time? (Please write them down)

_____

_____

_____

_____

3. If you were to die tomorrow would you be satisfied by having this worry consuming your last bit of precious time?

_____

_____

_____

_____

4. What else could this situation be teaching you?

_____

_____

_____

_____

Once you have discovered that the problem will subside within x amount of years, or the time frame you have chosen, you will already have a huge psychological advantage. When your mind perceives that the pain has no end in sight the intimidation of living forever with heart wrenching pain will be excruciating.

Imagine that you are the unlucky recipient that has to go through the experience of one of your family members, for example your mom, being kidnapped. The greatest fear for you will be whether or not you get to see her again. If the police, God forbid, find her lifeless body on the side of the road then you can at least begin to grieve her departure.

Though without the closure that your mom is not suffering will eat you alive.

A friend of mine loves telling this one story of his last break-up. His girlfriend phoned him up and said; "It's over Timmy." He was shocked. He pleaded with her not to end the fantastic 2 months they have spent together, but she refused. Just before she hung up he asked; "Why Stef, just tell me why?" "Because you forgot my birthday dumbass." – She said and smashed the phone down.

A massive smile crossed his face as he giggled to himself; "Mental note Timmy, remember you next girlfriends birthday." This example again shows that once we have closure we can move on easier. Knowing the Stef broke up with him for a specific reason allows him to learn a lesson and move on.

Ask these questions to get clarity on the problem and to understand its severity. Is it really deserving of your happiness or is there something else that your time is better suited for?

4. THE GRATITUDE OF 3

Write down 3 things that you can be grateful for today.

#	Gratitude
1.	
2.	
3.	

There is a profound TedxTalk by Shawn Achor, The Happiness Advantage, which describes the power of gratitude – appreciating what you have. After watching his fifteen minute presentation my mind went into a frenzy of contemplation around the idea of gratitude.

I started looking at my work colleges around me. All of them were constantly upset, stressed and miserable. My one work friend came into the office as angry as all hell; "My new born has kept me up all night." – He screamed. Just six months prior this man was the most excited father-to-be I have ever seen. Everyone around me, including myself, took what we had in their lives for granted. The blessings would come and the happiness would disappear.

Shawn Achor devised a very simple way to change our unappreciative mind-sets to ones that acknowledges blessings. The task is simple, every morning when you wake up think of three things that you are grateful for and write them down on a small pad.

You will probably start off with material blessings; I have a home, a car and a good job but as time progresses the blessings you count will have more fulfilment worth; I have a loving family, good health and I am blessed to live another day. Let the habit of gratitude form and watch your life change before your eyes.

5. It is Possible – The How question?

In David Schwartz's book, The Secret to Thinking Big, he explains that as soon as we see a goal as impossible our mind switches off to looking for opportunities to achieve it. The concept is simple, whenever you are faced with a challenging situation ask yourself the following question; if it were possible to complete said challenge how would it be possible?

1. How could you be happy right now?

    _____
    _____
    _____
    _____

2. How could you be motivated to achieve a specific goal right now?

    _____
    _____
    _____
    _____

3. How could you see a situation in a different way that helps you remain positive?

    _____
    _____
    _____
    _____

4. If you knew you couldn't fail how would your life look like in 5 years' time?

    _____
    _____
    _____
    _____

Using your mind to sift through possibilities may seem a little farfetched at first but think about this quickly, in this day and age we are constantly bombarded with information from hundreds of TV programs to millions of web pages and surplus amounts of social media activity. Our minds have to sift through all of that information because it is not possible to consume everything, therefore our minds select what to take in dependant on our interests.

If I like a specific girl I will make sure to see her Facebook posts for example. So using your mind to selectively sift through objects is very normal and something that we practise every day... now it's about using that powerful sifting ability to our advantage.

When we believe things to be possible or impossible our minds will come up with reasons to prove us right. If you believe that running under four minutes a mile is impossible your mind will say things like; "You haven't ever trained." "It takes so many years of dedication." "You're a little old and missed the boat." Etc. All providing facts to your belief.

Though if you were to believe that running under four minutes is possible your mind might react with the following; "It's been done before." "Our bodies are capable of running that fast." "If I dedicate myself to a training program and get a mentor it can be done."

You will come up with ideas on how to make it a reality. As soon as you believe things to be possible, or at least ask the question if it were possible how it would be accomplished... then your mind will go into a frantic frenzy of ideas on how to bring what you desire into your life.

Here is a quick example of the power of how in my life; I began the journey of a #1000ActsOfKindness in March 2013 with the hope that I could achieve 1000 acts in a year and nine months. I went on ski holiday to France with my dad and sister nearing the end of April. With my calculation I would have needed to complete fifty acts by that stage to ensure I was on track with completing my 1000 acts, though I had disappointingly only completed six.

I was totally dissatisfied and my mind reverted to the comfortable thoughts that it's impossible and that I shouldn't carry on. I was in the midst of reading David Schwartz's Thinking Big book and came across the HOW question. I related it to my situation and the question went as follows; If it were possible for me to do a #1000ActsOfKindness by the end of 2016 how would that be possible?

I sat in anticipation for a few minutes as some mediocre ideas came to mind, though nothing life changing. I was disappointed as this didn't give me the immediate relieve I was hoping for and I didn't see this approach as being helpful.

I placed the book down and got ready to enjoy some high-speed downward slopes with my dad. After three hours of intense enjoyment cruising around, we retired to a slope side restaurant. My dad and sister entered the restaurant rapidly and discovered a cute bench outside, sat and considered what to order.

I decided to run to the toilet first. On my way to the toilet I saw some rubbish lying on the ground, something I hadn't often taken note of before. I picked up the rubbish and threw it away on passage to the toilet, it was no extra work and if I didn't do it probably no one else would of. I arrived back at the table and my dad congratulated me on my act of kindness; "Well done Laurens, that was very kind of you."

I looked back in amazement at the place where the rubbish resided and realised my dad was right. That was an act of kindness. I know it sounds silly but I never pictured throwing someone else's rubbish away as an act of kindness but it was. I thought you have to give someone money in order to make a difference in the world.

My mind-set completely changed that day as I saw opportunity to do acts of kindness that I had never before even thought of. I smiled at people, opened the door for ladies to walk through before me and gave compliments to people who seemed down. All of these small gestures that I had never even contemplated as a suitable act of kindness. I give all the credit to The Secret of Thinking Big. As said in his book, once you ask the question your mind will come up with solutions to solve the problem.

Before the ski trip I was thinking about how it was impossible to reach #1000ActsOfKindness and so my mind went to work to prove me right and therefore I only saw opportunity to do six acts in one and a half months. Though when I contemplated that completing #1000ActsOfKindness was possible then ideas started to come to me.

It might not come in the form you expect, I was expecting a thousand great ideas after asking the question but it doesn't always work that way. Sometimes the answer comes when you least expect it. At least give your mind the opportunity to come up with some ideas to solve your problem, using the HOW.

6. The art of Comparison

To understand the true power of the art of comparison try this comparisons in your own life and see how different the perspectives can be.

1. Compare your wealth to that of Bill Gates. How does that make you feel?

    _____
    _____
    _____
    _____

2. Compare your wealth to that of Steven; a homeless hermit providing for his family with +/- R20 donations from roadside begging. How does that change the way you see your life?

_____

_____

_____

_____

It's obvious that in the first scenario you would have felt like you have a long way to go, Bill Gate's has stuck at rich and your wealth in comparison is pretty low. The second scenario will most likely be as revealing as the first in that you are blessed with what you currently have.

Your choice of comparison will determine the way in which you view your life. Choosing an unrealistic comparison like my sister, Julie, who compared her speaking ability with me who has been speaking for over one and a half years doesn't create a positive vision in her life, does it? We get to choose the person we want to compare ourselves with, and it will determine the way we see ourselves.

7. EVERYTHING HAPPENS FOR A REASON

Take a current challenging situation that you are experiencing and filter it through the following questions;

1. What could the reason be for this experience?

_____

_____

_____

_____

2. What lesson could I learn from this experience?

_____

_____

_____

_____

3. Is this experience going to repeat itself? Could I prepare better next time for it? How?

_____

_____

_____

_____

4. Remember the last time you went through a tough time, looking back now was there a reason for it happening? What was the reason? Has it helped you to make better decision today?

_____

_____

_____

_____

8. WORKING IN YOUR CIRCLE

Take a current situation where you feel out of control of the outcome and filter it through the following questions;

1. Who are you surrounding yourself with and what are their limiting beliefs? Are you adopting their baggage?

    _____
    _____
    _____
    _____

2. What can you do to make your goal become reality?

    _____
    _____
    _____
    _____

3. Break-up your goal into chunks of what you can control and what you can't control. Goal example; losing weight

Priority	Can Control	Can't control	Alternative Action
E.G. 4	Going to the gym	Gym being open	Check the times on the gym's website

Once you have defined what you can control, prioritize it so it will get done. What you cannot control see if there is alternative actions that you can control in order to ensure its completion.

9. Apologising

It was the end of year function for my department and due to high-workloads and serious stress burdens the executives decided to take us away on a beautiful day retreat to an estate, dam side where one of them stayed and had access to sport boats, golf carts and impeccable food services.

The team excitedly left together with the Gautrain and made their way to the executives pad. One of the team leaders, Wilma, a sweet German lady who was seen as the financial guru brought her daughter with to the festive day. Her daughter, Aqilha, had just turned eighteen and had her final matric exams coming up... she was stressed.

Aqilha comes from an Afrikaans-less background and therefore feared that exam the most. She overheard me speaking to one of my Afrikaans colleagues and was surprised at how well an English boy could speak Afrikaans. What she didn't know is that I had four years of Afrikaans fearfully drilled into me in my University and residence days.

She opened up conversation with complimenting my Afrikaans ability and soon went onto asking me for help with her exam coming up. I think she asked me for help and not the other Afrikaans employees because I was nearest to her age and she felt she could relate with me better. I happily agreed as coaching and mentoring is a passion of mine, even though I don't think I'm that qualified to mentor the Afrikaans subject.

Wilma and I sat down and correlated diaries in order to find a suitable day for her to bring Aqilha into the office. My suggestion of next week Wednesday was politely shut down as Aqilha had school Wednesday to Friday. The only available days were Monday and Tuesday next week. I checked my diary and saw that Monday I was not going to be in the office as I was away at the sea, so Tuesday was nailed down as the day of reckoning.

What I hadn't remembered was that on Tuesday I would be flying back from the sea and therefore it would be impossible for me to be in the office, but I didn't put that into my diary. A few days later and I was blissfully unaware arriving at Oliver Tambo Airport embraced by my kind sister who agreed to pick me up. It was around twelve pm when I entered her car.

She asked me; "Would you like to grab some lunch with me?" "Sounds great, I've got nowhere else to be." – I said unknowingly. Around three pm I arrived home, dropped the bags and headed straight to my computer to quickly catch up on the day's emails. That's when my heart sunk into my stomach. The first email that I received that morning was from Wilma with the subject title: Aqilha is here with me.

This was a fundamental error in judgement from me as Wilma was a particularly powerful and influential person in the corporate game, she was also someone that I was hoping to build a mentorship relationship with specifically from a financial investment standpoint. I saw her number in the email signature line and called it immediately.

She picked up the phone unknowing that it was me; "Hi, it's Wilma speaking." – She said in a joyously. "Hi Wilma, its Laurens here." – I replied cowardly. "Oh, it's *YOU*." – She snared in reply, and so began the series of intense and genuine apologises from my side sprinkled with convictions that everything was my fault.

By the end of the array of sorry's and accepting fault she seemed to have cooled down a little and ended the reasonable stern conversation with a light hearted joke; "It's ok Laurens, but Aqilha is going to kick your ass when she sees you." – Wilma jokingly said. "Thanks for understanding Wilma. If there is anything I can do to make up for it please let me know? I promise not to let this type of negligence happen again." – I said.

I used three powerful techniques to defuse the situation from an aggressive fight to a mediocre disagreement. The first was to genuinely apologise right away, in this case it was easy because it was undoubtedly my fault, and this immediately put Wilma in a more passive mode because she didn't need to prove that I made the mistake.

The next technique was to accept blame fully, and again it was easy in this case because it was my fault, but even if it wasn't it again takes the wind out of the angry persons sails as they again don't have to fight for being right. I tell you this story to shed light on how easy it can be to rectify a mistake. Anyone will gladly accept an honest, genuine apology peppered with a few *it was all my fault* comments.

The final technique was the last line I used; please let me know how to make it up to you and this type of negligence will never happen again. This shows that you are trying to make right the wrong and also that you have learnt a valuable lesson. Very few mistakes cannot be resolved using the simple process described above.

The steps of apologising;

1. Genuinely apologise for the mistake.
2. Accept the blame and absorb the faults made, even if you are not in the wrong this is a strong ingredient to rebuilding the trust and the relationship.
3. Ask if there is anything that you can do to make up for the mistake and that you will never let this specific mistake happen again.

We cannot please everyone and we will undoubtedly offend people along the way. Living in fear to please everyone is a battle not worth your time. Everyone will accept a genuine apology. So learn to apologize and go about living life to the best of your ability, when the opportunity to say sorry comes TAKE IT.

As Steve Maraboli said; "We all make mistakes, have struggles, and even regret things in our past. But we are not our mistakes, we are not our struggles, and we are here NOW with the power to shape our day and our future as we want." Use your mistakes to guide you not to define you.

10. Facing the Fear

Take a current situation that you is causing your fear filter it through the following questions;

1. What is the worst case scenario? Could you come back from it? How?

_____

_____

_____

_____

2. What is the potential payoff for breaking through the fear?

_____

_____

_____

_____

3. Have other people done what you want to do? Is it possible?

_____

_____

_____

_____

4. What are you going to do today to fight your fear? What are your actions cures to fighting the disease of fear?

_____

_____

_____

_____

GOAL SETTING EXERCISES

SETTING SMART GOALS

The first step to achieving big goals is to dream big.

Within each of the blocks below put 3 outrageous goals that you would like to achieve in each of the following areas; Mental

- Mental
- Physical
- Spiritual
- Social
- Work life

You don't need to know how they will come to past, this is an exercise to build up your creativity with dream setting.

Sphere	Outrageous Goal
E.G. Social	Have lunch with Oprah Winfrey

Congratulations, you have dreamt big and I hope you enjoyed the liberating feeling of living without obstacles. The next step is to now create an actionable plan going forward to achieve each of the pre-mentioned goals. Please write down one smaller goal that you would like to achieve, for example; to lose 10kg, watch less than 2 hours of TV per day... whatever is relevant in your life.

1. Current goal

_____

_____

_____

_____

Let's start by making this a SMART goal and then you can, in your own time, create an action plan for the above outrageous goals.

SPECIFIC

1. What do I want to accomplish? (Specificity is key – 10 Kilograms)

_____

_____

_____

_____

2. Specific reasons, purpose or benefits of accomplishing the goal. (The why that is going to drive motivation in the tough times)

_____

_____

_____

_____

3. Who is involved? (Would you need a coach)

_____

_____

_____

_____

4. Identify the location needed to achieve your goal? (Gym, at home)

_____

_____

_____

_____

5. Are there any constraints/requirements? (Time, money)

_____

_____

_____

_____

MEASURABLE

1. What quantity can you put on your goal? (10, 15, 20 kg)

_____

_____

_____

_____

2. How often would you need to DO something? (2, 3, 4 times a week to the gym)

_____

_____

_____

_____

3. When will you know that you have achieved your goal? (I have lost 10 kg by this time)

_____

_____

_____

_____

ATTAINABLE

1. In your current capacity can you achieve the goal?

_____

_____

_____

_____

2. If the answer to the above question is no then can you break the goal up into smaller portions? Can you achieve the smaller portions?

_____

_____

_____

_____

RELEVANT

1. Does this seem worthwhile?_____.
2. Is this the right time?_____.
3. Does this match your other efforts/needs?_____.

4. Are you the right person?_____.

5. Is it applicable in the current socio-economic-technical environment?

TIME-BOUND

1. By when can this goal be achieved?.

_____

_____

_____

_____

2. What can you do six months from now?

_____

_____

_____

_____

3. What can you do six weeks from now?

_____

_____

_____

_____

4. What can you do today?

_____

_____

_____

_____

REFERENCES

Most of the book's content is a culmination of coaching that I received as well as the books that I have read. Below are the books that served me most while writing this book.

Les Brown – 'Live Your Dreams'
Stephen R. Covey – '7 Habits of Highly Effective People'
David J. Schwartz – 'The Magic of Thinking Big'
Rhonda Byrne – 'The Secret'
Tim Ferris – 'The 4 Hour Work Week'
Shawn Achor – 'The Happiness Advantage'
Tony Robbins – 'Get The Edge'

Printed in the United States
By Bookmasters